60 Banana Recipes for Home

By: Kelly Johnson

Table of Contents

Breakfast and Brunch:

- Banana Pancakes
- Banana Walnut Muffins
- Banana Bread French Toast
- Banana Oatmeal
- Banana Smoothie Bowl
- Banana Nutella Crepes
- Banana Waffles
- Banana Foster Oatmeal
- Banana Chia Seed Pudding
- Banana and Almond Butter Toast

Snacks and Appetizers:

- Baked Banana Chips
- Banana Salsa with Cinnamon Chips
- Banana Guacamole
- Banana and Peanut Butter Energy Bites
- Banana Hummus
- Grilled Banana Skewers
- Banana Avocado Spring Rolls
- Banana and Cheese Quesadillas
- Banana Bruschetta
- Banana and Yogurt Dip

Desserts:

- Classic Banana Bread
- Banana Cream Pie
- Banana Split Sundae
- Chocolate Dipped Banana Pops
- Banana Pudding
- Banana Foster
- Banana Tiramisu
- Banana Ice Cream
- Banana Cheesecake

- Banana Fritters

Drinks:

- Banana Smoothie
- Banana Milkshake
- Banana Berry Smoothie
- Banana Coffee Smoothie
- Banana and Coconut Water Cooler
- Banana Lassi
- Banana Mojito
- Banana and Strawberry Lemonade
- Banana Colada
- Banana Iced Tea

Breads and Pastries:

- Banana Zucchini Bread
- Banana Blueberry Muffins
- Banana Chocolate Chip Scones
- Banana Cinnamon Rolls
- Banana Cranberry Bread
- Banana Nut Bread Pudding
- Banana Date Muffins
- Banana Cream Cheese Danish
- Banana Pecan Sticky Buns
- Banana Streusel Coffee Cake

Breakfast and Brunch:

- Grilled Banana and Chicken Skewers
- Banana and Ham Breakfast Burrito
- Banana and Bacon Stuffed French Toast
- Banana and Shrimp Lettuce Wraps
- Banana and Quinoa Stuffed Peppers
- Spicy Banana and Chicken Curry
- Banana and Black Bean Quesadillas
- Banana and Avocado Salad
- Banana and Cucumber Sushi Rolls
- Banana and Goat Cheese Crostini

Breakfast and Brunch:

Banana Pancakes

Ingredients:

- 2 ripe bananas, mashed
- 2 cups all-purpose flour
- 2 tablespoons sugar
- 2 teaspoons baking powder
- 1/2 teaspoon salt
- 1 1/2 cups milk
- 2 large eggs
- 1/4 cup unsalted butter, melted
- 1 teaspoon vanilla extract
- Optional: Sliced bananas, chopped nuts, or chocolate chips for topping

Instructions:

In a large mixing bowl, whisk together the mashed bananas, flour, sugar, baking powder, and salt.
In a separate bowl, whisk together the milk, eggs, melted butter, and vanilla extract.
Pour the wet ingredients into the dry ingredients and stir until just combined. Be careful not to overmix; it's okay if there are a few lumps.
Heat a griddle or non-stick skillet over medium heat. Lightly grease the surface with butter or cooking spray.
Scoop 1/4 cup portions of the batter onto the griddle for each pancake. Cook until bubbles form on the surface, then flip and cook the other side until golden brown.
Repeat until all the batter is used.
Serve the pancakes warm, topped with sliced bananas, chopped nuts, chocolate chips, or your favorite pancake toppings.
Optional: Drizzle with maple syrup or honey for added sweetness.

Enjoy your delicious banana pancakes! Feel free to customize the recipe by adding your favorite toppings or incorporating whole wheat flour for a healthier option.

Banana Walnut Muffins

Ingredients:

- 2 to 3 ripe bananas, mashed
- 1/2 cup unsalted butter, melted
- 1 teaspoon vanilla extract
- 1/2 cup granulated sugar
- 1/4 cup brown sugar, packed
- 1 large egg
- 1 1/2 cups all-purpose flour
- 1 teaspoon baking powder
- 1/2 teaspoon baking soda
- 1/2 teaspoon salt
- 1/2 teaspoon ground cinnamon
- 1/2 cup chopped walnuts
- Optional: 1/2 cup chocolate chips

Instructions:

Preheat your oven to 350°F (175°C). Line a muffin tin with paper liners or grease the cups.
In a large bowl, mash the ripe bananas with a fork.
Add the melted butter to the mashed bananas and mix well.
Stir in the vanilla extract, granulated sugar, and brown sugar until well combined.
Add the egg and mix until smooth.
In a separate bowl, whisk together the flour, baking powder, baking soda, salt, and ground cinnamon.
Gradually add the dry ingredients to the wet ingredients, mixing until just combined. Be careful not to overmix.
Fold in the chopped walnuts and, if desired, chocolate chips.
Spoon the batter into the muffin cups, filling each about 2/3 full.
Bake in the preheated oven for 18-20 minutes or until a toothpick inserted into the center of a muffin comes out clean.
Allow the muffins to cool in the tin for a few minutes before transferring them to a wire rack to cool completely.
Enjoy your delicious banana walnut muffins!

Feel free to customize the recipe by adding other mix-ins like raisins, dried fruits, or shredded coconut. These muffins make for a delightful breakfast or snack.

Banana Bread French Toast

Ingredients:

For Banana Bread:

- 3 ripe bananas, mashed
- 1/2 cup unsalted butter, melted
- 1 teaspoon vanilla extract
- 1 cup granulated sugar
- 1 1/2 cups all-purpose flour
- 1 teaspoon baking soda
- 1/4 teaspoon salt

For French Toast:

- 4-6 slices of your homemade banana bread (allow it to cool before using)
- 3 large eggs
- 1/2 cup milk
- 1 teaspoon vanilla extract
- Butter or cooking spray for greasing the pan
- Optional toppings: Sliced bananas, maple syrup, powdered sugar, chopped nuts

Instructions:

For Banana Bread:

Preheat your oven to 350°F (175°C). Grease and flour a loaf pan.
In a large bowl, mash the ripe bananas.
Add melted butter, vanilla extract, and sugar to the mashed bananas. Mix well.
In a separate bowl, whisk together the flour, baking soda, and salt.
Combine the wet and dry ingredients, mixing until just combined.
Pour the batter into the prepared loaf pan and bake for about 60-70 minutes or until a toothpick inserted into the center comes out clean.
Allow the banana bread to cool completely before slicing.

For French Toast:

In a shallow dish, whisk together eggs, milk, and vanilla extract.
Heat a griddle or skillet over medium heat and grease with butter or cooking spray.
Dip each slice of banana bread into the egg mixture, coating both sides evenly.
Place the dipped slices on the hot griddle and cook until golden brown on each side, usually 2-3 minutes per side.
Once cooked, transfer the French toast slices to a serving plate.
Serve with optional toppings like sliced bananas, maple syrup, powdered sugar, or chopped nuts.
Enjoy your delicious Banana Bread French Toast!

This recipe combines the flavors of banana bread with the classic French toast, creating a delightful and comforting breakfast.

Banana Oatmeal

Ingredients:

- 1 cup old-fashioned rolled oats
- 2 cups milk (dairy or plant-based)
- 1-2 ripe bananas, mashed
- 1 teaspoon vanilla extract
- 1/2 teaspoon ground cinnamon
- Pinch of salt
- Optional toppings: Sliced bananas, chopped nuts, honey, or maple syrup

Instructions:

In a medium-sized saucepan, combine the oats, milk, mashed bananas, vanilla extract, ground cinnamon, and a pinch of salt.
Place the saucepan over medium heat and bring the mixture to a simmer.
Reduce the heat to low and simmer, stirring occasionally, for about 5-7 minutes or until the oats are cooked to your desired consistency.
Once the oatmeal is cooked, remove the saucepan from the heat.
Serve the banana oatmeal in bowls and top with sliced bananas, chopped nuts, and a drizzle of honey or maple syrup if desired.
Stir the toppings into the oatmeal and enjoy your delicious and comforting banana oatmeal breakfast!

Feel free to customize this recipe by adding your favorite toppings such as berries, shredded coconut, or a dollop of yogurt. This wholesome and hearty breakfast will keep you energized throughout the morning.

Banana Smoothie Bowl

Ingredients:

For the Smoothie Base:

- 2 ripe bananas, frozen
- 1 cup plain Greek yogurt
- 1/2 cup milk (dairy or plant-based)
- 1 tablespoon honey or maple syrup (optional for sweetness)
- 1/2 teaspoon vanilla extract

Toppings:

- Sliced bananas
- Fresh berries (strawberries, blueberries, raspberries)
- Granola
- Chia seeds
- Shredded coconut
- Nuts (almonds, walnuts, or your choice)
- Drizzle of honey or maple syrup

Instructions:

In a blender, combine the frozen bananas, Greek yogurt, milk, honey or maple syrup (if using), and vanilla extract.
Blend until smooth and creamy. If the mixture is too thick, you can add a little more milk to achieve the desired consistency.
Pour the smoothie into a bowl.
Arrange your desired toppings on the smoothie base. Get creative and make a visually appealing design with your favorite ingredients.
Drizzle honey or maple syrup on top for extra sweetness if desired.
Serve immediately and enjoy your delicious and colorful banana smoothie bowl!

Feel free to experiment with different toppings based on your preferences. You can add superfoods like acai berries or spirulina for an extra nutritional boost. This smoothie bowl is not only tasty but also packed with vitamins, fiber, and protein.

Banana Nutella Crepes

Ingredients:

For the Crepes:

- 1 cup all-purpose flour
- 2 large eggs
- 1 cup milk
- 1/2 cup water
- 2 tablespoons melted butter
- 1 tablespoon sugar
- 1/2 teaspoon vanilla extract
- Pinch of salt

For Filling and Topping:

- Ripe bananas, sliced
- Nutella (as much as desired)
- Chopped nuts (e.g., hazelnuts, almonds, or walnuts)
- Powdered sugar for dusting

Instructions:

Prepare the Crepe Batter:
- In a blender, combine flour, eggs, milk, water, melted butter, sugar, vanilla extract, and a pinch of salt.
- Blend until the batter is smooth. Let it rest for about 15-20 minutes.

Cook the Crepes:
- Heat a non-stick skillet or crepe pan over medium heat.
- Pour a small amount of batter into the center of the pan, swirling it around to spread thinly.
- Cook for about 1-2 minutes until the edges start to lift, then flip and cook for an additional 1-2 minutes on the other side. Repeat until all the batter is used.

Assemble the Crepes:
- Spread Nutella on one half of each crepe.
- Add sliced bananas on top of the Nutella.

Fold and Serve:

- Fold the crepes in half and then in half again to form a triangle.
- Place the crepes on a serving plate.

Top and Garnish:
- Drizzle additional Nutella over the top.
- Sprinkle chopped nuts over the crepes.
- Dust with powdered sugar for a finishing touch.

Serve and Enjoy:
- Serve the Banana Nutella Crepes warm and enjoy your delicious treat!

Feel free to get creative with additional toppings such as whipped cream, berries, or a scoop of vanilla ice cream. These crepes make for a delightful dessert or indulgent breakfast.

Banana Waffles

Ingredients:

- 2 cups all-purpose flour
- 2 tablespoons sugar
- 1 tablespoon baking powder
- 1/2 teaspoon salt
- 2 ripe bananas, mashed
- 2 large eggs
- 1 3/4 cups milk
- 1/3 cup unsalted butter, melted
- 1 teaspoon vanilla extract
- Optional: Chopped nuts, sliced bananas, or chocolate chips for added texture and flavor

Instructions:

Preheat your Waffle Maker:
- Preheat your waffle maker according to its manufacturer's instructions.

Prepare the Dry Ingredients:
- In a large mixing bowl, whisk together the flour, sugar, baking powder, and salt.

Mix the Wet Ingredients:
- In a separate bowl, mash the ripe bananas and whisk in the eggs, milk, melted butter, and vanilla extract until well combined.

Combine Wet and Dry Ingredients:
- Pour the wet ingredients into the dry ingredients and stir until just combined. Be careful not to overmix; a few lumps are okay.

Add Optional Ingredients:
- If desired, fold in chopped nuts, sliced bananas, or chocolate chips for added flavor and texture.

Cook the Waffles:
- Lightly grease the waffle maker with cooking spray or a small amount of melted butter.
- Pour the batter onto the preheated waffle maker according to its size guidelines.

Cook Until Golden Brown:

- Close the waffle maker and cook until the waffles are golden brown and crisp.

Serve Warm:
- Remove the waffles from the maker and serve them warm.

Optional Toppings:
- Top your banana waffles with additional sliced bananas, a drizzle of maple syrup, a dollop of whipped cream, or any of your favorite toppings.

Enjoy:
- Enjoy your delicious homemade banana waffles!

These banana waffles make for a delightful breakfast or brunch option. Customize them with your favorite toppings and enjoy the sweet, comforting flavors.

Banana Foster Oatmeal

Ingredients:

- 1 cup old-fashioned rolled oats
- 2 ripe bananas, sliced
- 2 tablespoons unsalted butter
- 1/4 cup brown sugar
- 1/4 teaspoon ground cinnamon
- 1/4 cup chopped pecans or walnuts (optional)
- 1 teaspoon vanilla extract
- Pinch of salt
- 1 1/2 cups milk (dairy or plant-based)
- Optional toppings: Sliced bananas, additional nuts, and a drizzle of honey or maple syrup

Instructions:

Prepare the Oatmeal Base:
- In a medium-sized saucepan, combine the oats, sliced bananas, and milk.

Cook the Oatmeal:
- Cook the oatmeal over medium heat, stirring occasionally, until it reaches your desired consistency.

Prepare the Banana Foster Topping:
- In a separate skillet, melt the butter over medium heat.

Add Sugar and Caramelize:
- Stir in the brown sugar and cinnamon until the sugar is dissolved.

Add Bananas and Nuts:
- Add the sliced bananas and chopped nuts (if using) to the skillet. Cook for 2-3 minutes until the bananas are softened and coated in the caramelized sugar mixture.

Add Vanilla and Salt:
- Stir in the vanilla extract and a pinch of salt. Cook for an additional 1-2 minutes.

Combine Oatmeal and Banana Foster:
- Pour the banana foster mixture over the cooked oatmeal and stir gently to combine.

Serve:

- Spoon the Banana Foster Oatmeal into bowls.

Add Toppings:
- Top with additional sliced bananas, nuts, and a drizzle of honey or maple syrup if desired.

Enjoy:
- Serve warm and enjoy your delicious and indulgent Banana Foster Oatmeal!

This oatmeal is a decadent and comforting breakfast that brings together the rich flavors of caramelized bananas and warm spices. It's a perfect treat for a special morning.

Banana Chia Seed Pudding

Ingredients:

- 1 ripe banana, mashed
- 1/4 cup chia seeds
- 1 cup milk (dairy or plant-based)
- 1/2 teaspoon vanilla extract
- 1 tablespoon honey or maple syrup (optional, for sweetness)
- Sliced bananas and chopped nuts for topping

Instructions:

Mash the Banana:
- In a bowl, mash the ripe banana with a fork until smooth.

Combine Ingredients:
- Add chia seeds, milk, vanilla extract, and honey or maple syrup (if using) to the mashed banana. Stir well to combine.

Let it Sit:
- Cover the bowl and refrigerate the mixture for at least 4 hours or overnight. This allows the chia seeds to absorb the liquid and create a pudding-like consistency.

Stir Again:
- After the initial refrigeration, give the mixture a good stir. If it's too thick, you can add a bit more milk to reach your desired consistency.

Serve:
- Spoon the banana chia seed pudding into serving glasses or bowls.

Top with Sliced Bananas and Nuts:
- Garnish with sliced bananas and chopped nuts.

Optional: Drizzle with Honey:
- If you like it sweeter, you can drizzle a bit of honey on top.

Enjoy:
- Serve chilled and enjoy your delicious and nutritious Banana Chia Seed Pudding!

Feel free to get creative with additional toppings like berries, shredded coconut, or a dollop of yogurt. This pudding is not only tasty but also packed with fiber, omega-3 fatty acids from chia seeds, and potassium from bananas, making it a wholesome and satisfying option.

Banana and Almond Butter Toast

Ingredients:

- 1-2 slices of whole-grain bread (toasted)
- 1 ripe banana, sliced
- 2 tablespoons almond butter
- Optional: Drizzle of honey or sprinkle of cinnamon

Instructions:

Toast the Bread:
- Toast the slices of whole-grain bread to your desired level of crispiness.

Spread Almond Butter:
- While the bread is still warm, spread a generous layer of almond butter on each slice.

Add Sliced Banana:
- Arrange the sliced bananas evenly over the almond butter.

Optional Toppings:
- Drizzle a bit of honey over the top or sprinkle a dash of cinnamon for extra flavor.

Serve:
- Place the banana and almond butter toast on a plate and serve immediately.

Enjoy:
- Enjoy your delicious and satisfying Banana and Almond Butter Toast!

This simple and nutritious toast combination provides a good balance of carbohydrates, healthy fats, and natural sweetness. It's a great way to fuel your day or satisfy a quick craving for something tasty.

Snacks and Appetizers:

Baked Banana Chips

Ingredients:

- 2-3 ripe bananas (slightly firm)
- Lemon juice (from 1 lemon)
- Optional: Cinnamon or honey for added flavor

Instructions:

Preheat the Oven:
- Preheat your oven to 200°F (93°C). Line a baking sheet with parchment paper.

Prepare the Bananas:
- Peel the bananas and thinly slice them into even rounds, about 1/8 to 1/4 inch thick.

Lemon Juice Coating:
- Place the banana slices in a bowl and toss them with lemon juice. The lemon juice helps prevent browning and adds a hint of citrus flavor.

Arrange on Baking Sheet:
- Arrange the banana slices in a single layer on the prepared baking sheet. Make sure the slices are not touching or overlapping.

Optional Flavoring:
- If desired, sprinkle the banana slices with a bit of cinnamon or drizzle them with honey for added flavor.

Bake in the Oven:
- Bake in the preheated oven for 2-3 hours or until the banana chips are crisp. Flip the banana slices halfway through the baking time to ensure even crispiness.

Check for Doneness:
- Keep an eye on the banana chips in the last hour of baking to prevent over-browning. The chips are ready when they are dry and have a golden color.

Cool:
- Allow the banana chips to cool completely on the baking sheet. They will continue to crisp up as they cool.

Store:
- Once cooled, store the banana chips in an airtight container to maintain their crispness.

Enjoy:
- Enjoy your homemade baked banana chips as a healthy snack!

These baked banana chips are a delicious alternative to store-bought snacks and are free from added sugars and preservatives. They're perfect for munching on the go or as a topping for yogurt and cereal.

Banana Salsa with Cinnamon Chips

Ingredients:

For Banana Salsa:

- 3 ripe bananas, diced
- 1 cup strawberries, diced
- 1 kiwi, peeled and diced
- 1 tablespoon fresh lime juice
- 2 tablespoons honey or maple syrup
- 1 tablespoon fresh mint, chopped

For Cinnamon Chips:

- 6-8 flour tortillas
- 2 tablespoons unsalted butter, melted
- 1/4 cup granulated sugar
- 1 teaspoon ground cinnamon

Instructions:

Preheat the Oven:
- Preheat your oven to 350°F (175°C).

Make Cinnamon Chips:
- Brush each tortilla with melted butter on both sides.
- In a small bowl, mix together sugar and ground cinnamon.
- Sprinkle the cinnamon-sugar mixture evenly over each tortilla.
- Stack the tortillas and cut them into wedges (like pizza slices).

Bake Cinnamon Chips:
- Arrange the tortilla wedges on a baking sheet in a single layer.
- Bake in the preheated oven for 8-10 minutes or until the chips are golden brown and crispy.

Prepare Banana Salsa:
- In a medium bowl, combine diced bananas, strawberries, kiwi, lime juice, honey or maple syrup, and chopped mint. Gently toss to coat.

Serve:

- Allow the cinnamon chips to cool slightly before serving.
- Serve the banana salsa in a bowl alongside the cinnamon chips.

Enjoy:
- Enjoy this refreshing and sweet Banana Salsa with Cinnamon Chips!

This combination offers a perfect balance of sweet and tangy flavors, and the crispy cinnamon chips add a delightful crunch. It's a fantastic dessert or snack option for gatherings or a sweet treat at home.

Banana Guacamole

Ingredients:

- 3 ripe avocados, peeled and mashed
- 2 ripe bananas, mashed
- 1/2 cup red onion, finely chopped
- 1/4 cup fresh cilantro, chopped
- 1-2 cloves garlic, minced
- 1 jalapeño, seeds removed and finely chopped (optional for heat)
- Juice of 2 limes
- Salt and pepper to taste
- Tortilla chips or sliced fruits for serving

Instructions:

Prepare Avocados and Bananas:
- Peel and pit the avocados, and mash them in a mixing bowl.
- Mash the ripe bananas separately and add them to the bowl with the avocados.

Add Ingredients:
- Add finely chopped red onion, minced garlic, chopped cilantro, and chopped jalapeño (if using) to the mashed avocados and bananas.

Seasoning:
- Squeeze the juice of two limes over the mixture.
- Season with salt and pepper to taste.

Mix Well:
- Gently mix all the ingredients together until well combined.

Chill:
- Cover the bowl with plastic wrap, ensuring it directly touches the surface of the guacamole to prevent browning.
- Refrigerate for at least 30 minutes to let the flavors meld.

Serve:
- Just before serving, give the banana guacamole a final gentle stir.
- Serve with tortilla chips or sliced fruits.

Enjoy:
- Enjoy this sweet and savory Banana Guacamole as a unique dip for your snacks or as a side dish.

This banana guacamole brings together the creamy texture of avocados with the natural sweetness of ripe bananas, creating a refreshing and unexpected flavor combination. It's perfect for a summer party or as a fun twist to your regular guacamole routine.

Banana and Peanut Butter Energy Bites

Ingredients:

- 2 ripe bananas, mashed
- 1 cup rolled oats
- 1/2 cup peanut butter (or any nut butter of your choice)
- 1/4 cup honey or maple syrup
- 1 teaspoon vanilla extract
- 1/2 cup shredded coconut (optional, for coating)
- 1/4 cup mini chocolate chips or chopped nuts (optional, for added texture)

Instructions:

Mash Bananas:
- In a mixing bowl, mash the ripe bananas with a fork until smooth.

Add Ingredients:
- Add rolled oats, peanut butter, honey or maple syrup, vanilla extract, and optional chocolate chips or nuts to the mashed bananas.

Mix Well:
- Mix all the ingredients until well combined.

Chill the Mixture:
- Place the mixture in the refrigerator for about 15-30 minutes to firm up slightly. This makes it easier to shape the energy bites.

Shape into Bites:
- Once chilled, take small portions of the mixture and roll them into bite-sized balls using your hands.

Optional Coating:
- If desired, roll the energy bites in shredded coconut for an extra layer of flavor and texture.

Chill Again:
- Place the energy bites on a tray lined with parchment paper and refrigerate for another 30 minutes to set.

Store:
- Store the banana and peanut butter energy bites in an airtight container in the refrigerator.

Enjoy:
- Grab a couple of these energy bites whenever you need a quick and nutritious snack!

These energy bites are not only delicious but also packed with fiber, healthy fats, and natural sweetness from the bananas. They make for a convenient and satisfying snack on the go.

Banana Hummus

Ingredients:

- 1 can (15 ounces) chickpeas, drained and rinsed
- 2 ripe bananas
- 1/4 cup tahini (sesame paste)
- 1/4 cup pure maple syrup or honey
- 2 tablespoons lemon juice
- 1 teaspoon vanilla extract
- 1/4 teaspoon ground cinnamon
- Pinch of salt
- Optional toppings: Sliced bananas, a drizzle of honey, or a sprinkle of cinnamon

Instructions:

Prepare Chickpeas:
- Drain and rinse the chickpeas thoroughly.

Blend Ingredients:
- In a food processor, combine the chickpeas, ripe bananas, tahini, maple syrup or honey, lemon juice, vanilla extract, ground cinnamon, and a pinch of salt.

Blend until Smooth:
- Blend the ingredients until you achieve a smooth and creamy consistency. You may need to scrape down the sides of the food processor to ensure everything is well incorporated.

Adjust Consistency:
- If the hummus is too thick, you can add a little water, one tablespoon at a time, until you reach your desired consistency.

Taste and Adjust Sweetness:
- Taste the hummus and adjust the sweetness by adding more maple syrup or honey if needed.

Serve:
- Transfer the banana hummus to a serving bowl.

Optional Toppings:
- Top with sliced bananas, a drizzle of honey, or a sprinkle of cinnamon for extra flavor.

Enjoy:

- Serve your banana hummus with fruit slices, crackers, or as a delicious spread on toast.

This sweet and creamy banana hummus is a delightful treat that can be enjoyed as a healthy snack or dessert. It's a great way to incorporate the natural sweetness of bananas into a savory dish.

Grilled Banana Skewers

Ingredients:

- Ripe bananas
- Wooden skewers, soaked in water for at least 30 minutes
- Honey or maple syrup (optional, for drizzling)
- Cinnamon (optional, for sprinkling)
- Vanilla ice cream (optional, for serving)

Instructions:

Prepare the Grill:
- Preheat your grill to medium-high heat.

Prepare the Bananas:
- Peel the ripe bananas and cut them into chunks, approximately 1 to 2 inches in size.

Assemble Skewers:
- Thread the banana chunks onto the soaked wooden skewers.

Grill the Skewers:
- Place the banana skewers on the preheated grill.

Grill Until Caramelized:
- Grill the banana skewers for about 2-3 minutes per side or until they are caramelized and have grill marks.

Optional: Drizzle and Sprinkle:
- Optional: While grilling or after removing from the grill, drizzle the grilled banana skewers with honey or maple syrup and sprinkle with cinnamon for added sweetness and flavor.

Serve:
- Remove the banana skewers from the grill and transfer them to a serving plate.

Optional: Serve with Ice Cream:
- For an extra treat, serve the grilled banana skewers with a scoop of vanilla ice cream.

Enjoy:
- Enjoy your delicious grilled banana skewers immediately while they're warm.

This simple grilled banana skewer recipe offers a delightful combination of caramelized sweetness from the bananas and a hint of smokiness from the grill. It's a quick and impressive dessert that's perfect for gatherings or a sweet treat after a barbecue.

Banana Avocado Spring Rolls

Ingredients:

For the Spring Rolls:

- Rice paper wrappers
- 2 ripe bananas, sliced
- 1 ripe avocado, sliced
- Fresh mint leaves
- Rice vermicelli noodles, cooked and cooled

For the Dipping Sauce:

- 1/4 cup creamy peanut butter
- 2 tablespoons soy sauce
- 1 tablespoon rice vinegar
- 1 tablespoon honey or maple syrup
- 1 teaspoon sesame oil
- 1 clove garlic, minced
- 1 teaspoon grated fresh ginger
- Water (as needed to adjust the consistency)

Instructions:

Prepare Rice Vermicelli:
- Cook the rice vermicelli noodles according to the package instructions. Once cooked, rinse them under cold water and set aside to cool.

Prepare Dipping Sauce:
- In a bowl, whisk together peanut butter, soy sauce, rice vinegar, honey or maple syrup, sesame oil, minced garlic, and grated ginger. If the sauce is too thick, you can add a little water to achieve the desired consistency.

Prepare Ingredients:
- Slice the ripe bananas and avocado. Arrange the banana slices, avocado slices, fresh mint leaves, and cooled rice vermicelli noodles in separate bowls for easy assembly.

Soak Rice Paper Wrappers:

- Fill a shallow dish with warm water. Dip each rice paper wrapper into the water for about 10-15 seconds or until softened.

Assemble Spring Rolls:
- Lay the softened rice paper wrapper on a clean surface.
- Place a few slices of banana and avocado, a handful of rice vermicelli noodles, and a few mint leaves in the center of the wrapper.

Roll the Spring Rolls:
- Fold in the sides of the rice paper and tightly roll up the filling, similar to a burrito.

Repeat:
- Repeat the process until all ingredients are used.

Serve with Dipping Sauce:
- Serve the banana avocado spring rolls with the prepared dipping sauce.

Enjoy:
- Enjoy these refreshing and fruity spring rolls as a light and tasty snack or appetizer.

These banana avocado spring rolls are a delightful combination of sweet and creamy, making them a unique and delicious treat. The dipping sauce adds a savory and nutty flavor that complements the freshness of the ingredients.

Banana and Cheese Quesadillas

Ingredients:

- Flour tortillas
- Ripe bananas, sliced
- Cheddar cheese, shredded (or any cheese of your choice)
- Butter or cooking spray for greasing the pan
- Optional: Honey or cinnamon for drizzling

Instructions:

Prepare Ingredients:
- Lay out the flour tortillas and have the sliced bananas and shredded cheese ready.

Assemble Quesadillas:
- Place a handful of shredded cheese on half of each tortilla.
- Arrange banana slices over the cheese.

Fold the Quesadillas:
- Fold the tortillas in half, covering the banana and cheese filling.

Cook on the Stovetop:
- Heat a skillet or griddle over medium heat. Add butter or use cooking spray to coat the surface.

Cook Quesadillas:
- Place the folded quesadillas on the hot skillet and cook for 2-3 minutes on each side or until the tortillas are golden brown and the cheese is melted.

Optional: Drizzle or Sprinkle:
- Optional: Drizzle honey over the top or sprinkle a bit of cinnamon for extra flavor.

Slice and Serve:
- Remove the quesadillas from the pan, let them cool for a moment, then slice into wedges.

Enjoy:
- Serve the banana and cheese quesadillas warm and enjoy this unique and delicious combination!

The sweet and savory contrast in these quesadillas makes them a tasty snack or even a quick and quirky dessert. The melted cheese adds a rich and gooey texture, while the banana provides natural sweetness. Feel free to get creative with additional toppings or serve them with a dollop of whipped cream or a scoop of vanilla ice cream for an extra treat.

Banana Bruschetta

Ingredients:

- Baguette or French bread, sliced
- Ripe bananas, sliced
- Cream cheese or mascarpone cheese
- Honey for drizzling
- Fresh mint leaves for garnish (optional)

Instructions:

Preheat the Oven:
- Preheat your oven to broil.

Slice and Toast the Bread:
- Arrange the baguette or French bread slices on a baking sheet. Place them under the broiler for 1-2 minutes, or until they are lightly toasted. Keep an eye on them to prevent burning.

Spread Cheese:
- Spread a layer of cream cheese or mascarpone cheese on each toasted bread slice.

Add Banana Slices:
- Place banana slices on top of the cheese-covered bread slices.

Drizzle with Honey:
- Drizzle honey generously over the banana slices.

Optional Garnish:
- Optionally, garnish each bruschetta with fresh mint leaves for a burst of freshness.

Serve:
- Arrange the banana bruschettas on a serving platter.

Enjoy:
- Serve immediately and enjoy this delightful and sweet twist on traditional bruschetta!

This banana bruschetta makes for a unique and elegant appetizer or dessert. The combination of creamy cheese, sweet bananas, and honey on crunchy toast creates a delightful flavor and texture contrast. It's a simple yet impressive treat for various occasions.

Banana and Yogurt Dip

Ingredients:

- 2 ripe bananas, mashed
- 1 cup Greek yogurt (or any yogurt of your choice)
- 1-2 tablespoons honey or maple syrup (adjust to taste)
- 1/2 teaspoon vanilla extract
- Optional toppings: Sliced bananas, berries, chopped nuts, or granola

Instructions:

Prepare Bananas:
- In a bowl, mash the ripe bananas with a fork until smooth.

Combine Ingredients:
- Add Greek yogurt, honey or maple syrup, and vanilla extract to the mashed bananas.

Mix Well:
- Stir the ingredients until well combined.

Adjust Sweetness:
- Taste the dip and adjust the sweetness by adding more honey or maple syrup if desired.

Chill:
- For optimal flavor, refrigerate the dip for at least 30 minutes to allow the flavors to meld.

Serve:
- Spoon the banana and yogurt dip into a serving bowl.

Optional Toppings:
- Top the dip with sliced bananas, berries, chopped nuts, or granola for added texture and flavor.

Enjoy:
- Serve as a dip for fruit slices, pretzels, or graham crackers, or enjoy it on its own.

This banana and yogurt dip is a nutritious and satisfying option for a light snack or dessert. The combination of creamy yogurt and sweet bananas creates a delightful flavor, and you can customize it with your favorite toppings for added variety.

Desserts:

Classic Banana Bread

Ingredients:

- 3 ripe bananas, mashed
- 1/3 cup unsalted butter, melted
- 1 teaspoon baking soda
- Pinch of salt
- 3/4 cup granulated sugar
- 1 large egg, beaten
- 1 teaspoon vanilla extract
- 1 1/2 cups all-purpose flour

Optional Add-ins:

- 1/2 cup chopped nuts (walnuts or pecans)
- 1/2 cup chocolate chips or raisins

Instructions:

Preheat the Oven:
- Preheat your oven to 350°F (175°C). Grease a 4x8 inch loaf pan.

Mash Bananas:
- In a mixing bowl, mash the ripe bananas with a fork or potato masher until smooth.

Add Melted Butter:
- Stir the melted butter into the mashed bananas.

Add Baking Soda and Salt:
- Add the baking soda and a pinch of salt to the banana mixture. Stir to combine.

Add Sugar, Egg, and Vanilla:
- Add the sugar, beaten egg, and vanilla extract to the banana mixture. Mix well.

Incorporate Flour:
- Stir in the flour until just incorporated. Be careful not to overmix.

Optional Add-ins:

- If desired, fold in chopped nuts, chocolate chips, or raisins.

Pour into Loaf Pan:
- Pour the batter into the greased loaf pan.

Bake:
- Bake in the preheated oven for 60-65 minutes or until a toothpick inserted into the center comes out clean.

Cool:
- Allow the banana bread to cool in the pan for about 10 minutes, then transfer it to a wire rack to cool completely.

Slice and Enjoy:
- Once cooled, slice the banana bread and enjoy!

This classic banana bread recipe is versatile, and you can customize it by adding your favorite mix-ins or enjoying it as is. It's perfect for breakfast, as a snack, or for satisfying your sweet cravings.

Banana Cream Pie

Ingredients:

For the Pie Crust:

- 1 1/2 cups graham cracker crumbs
- 1/3 cup granulated sugar
- 6 tablespoons unsalted butter, melted

For the Banana Filling:

- 3 large ripe bananas, sliced
- 1 1/2 cups whole milk
- 1/2 cup heavy cream
- 1 cup granulated sugar
- 1/3 cup all-purpose flour
- 1/4 teaspoon salt
- 4 large egg yolks, beaten
- 2 tablespoons unsalted butter
- 1 teaspoon vanilla extract

For the Whipped Cream Topping:

- 1 cup heavy cream
- 2 tablespoons powdered sugar
- 1 teaspoon vanilla extract

Instructions:

Preheat the Oven:
- Preheat your oven to 375°F (190°C).

Make the Pie Crust:
- In a bowl, combine graham cracker crumbs, sugar, and melted butter. Press the mixture into the bottom and up the sides of a 9-inch pie dish. Bake the crust for about 8-10 minutes until golden brown. Allow it to cool completely.

Prepare the Banana Filling:
- In a saucepan, combine sugar, flour, and salt. Gradually whisk in the milk and heavy cream until smooth.
- Place the saucepan over medium heat, stirring constantly until the mixture thickens and comes to a boil.

Temper the Eggs:
- Place the beaten egg yolks in a separate bowl. Slowly pour about 1/2 cup of the hot milk mixture into the egg yolks while whisking continuously. This tempers the eggs and prevents them from curdling.

Combine and Cook:
- Pour the tempered egg mixture back into the saucepan with the remaining hot milk mixture. Cook for an additional 2 minutes, stirring constantly.

Remove from Heat:
- Remove the saucepan from heat and stir in the butter and vanilla extract until well combined.

Assemble the Pie:
- Arrange a layer of sliced bananas in the cooled pie crust. Pour the custard mixture over the bananas.

Chill:
- Place the pie in the refrigerator and let it chill for at least 4 hours or until set.

Make Whipped Cream Topping:
- In a separate bowl, whip the heavy cream, powdered sugar, and vanilla extract until stiff peaks form.

Serve:
- Spread the whipped cream over the chilled banana filling.

Slice and Enjoy:
- Slice the banana cream pie and enjoy this delicious and classic dessert!

This banana cream pie is a perfect blend of creamy filling, fresh bananas, and a buttery graham cracker crust. It's a crowd-pleaser and a great choice for any occasion.

Banana Split Sundae

Ingredients:

- Ripe bananas, split lengthwise
- Vanilla ice cream
- Chocolate ice cream
- Strawberry ice cream
- Chocolate syrup
- Strawberry sauce or fresh strawberries, sliced
- Pineapple topping or fresh pineapple chunks
- Whipped cream
- Chopped nuts (such as walnuts or almonds)
- Maraschino cherries

Instructions:

Prepare the Bananas:
- Peel and split the ripe bananas lengthwise.

Assemble the Banana Split:
- Place the banana halves in a dish or on a banana split boat.

Add Scoops of Ice Cream:
- Add scoops of vanilla, chocolate, and strawberry ice cream between the banana halves.

Add Toppings:
- Drizzle chocolate syrup over the chocolate ice cream.
- Add strawberry sauce or scatter fresh strawberry slices over the strawberry ice cream.
- Spoon pineapple topping or place fresh pineapple chunks on the vanilla ice cream.

Whipped Cream:
- Generously dollop whipped cream over the entire banana split.

Chopped Nuts:
- Sprinkle chopped nuts, such as walnuts or almonds, over the whipped cream.

Cherries on Top:
- Top the banana split with maraschino cherries.

Serve Immediately:

- Serve the Banana Split Sundae immediately while the ice cream is still cold and the toppings are fresh.

Enjoy:
- Dive into this delightful Banana Split Sundae, enjoying the combination of flavors and textures.

Feel free to customize the toppings based on your preferences. You can also add other toppings like shredded coconut, sprinkles, or caramel sauce for extra indulgence. The Banana Split Sundae is a classic dessert that's perfect for sharing or as a special treat for yourself.

Chocolate Dipped Banana Pops

Ingredients:

- Ripe bananas, peeled and cut in half
- Dark or milk chocolate, chopped (about 8 ounces)
- Toppings of your choice (chopped nuts, shredded coconut, sprinkles, crushed graham crackers, etc.)
- Wooden popsicle sticks or skewers

Instructions:

Prepare Banana Halves:
- Peel the ripe bananas and cut them in half. Insert a wooden popsicle stick or skewer into the cut end of each banana half, creating banana pops.

Freeze:
- Place the banana pops on a tray lined with parchment paper and freeze them for at least 2 hours or until they are firm.

Melt Chocolate:
- In a microwave-safe bowl or using a double boiler, melt the chocolate until smooth. Stir the chocolate every 20-30 seconds if using a microwave to prevent burning.

Dip the Bananas:
- Dip each frozen banana pop into the melted chocolate, ensuring the banana is well coated. Allow excess chocolate to drip off.

Add Toppings:
- While the chocolate is still wet, roll the chocolate-coated banana pops in your chosen toppings. Try chopped nuts, shredded coconut, sprinkles, or crushed graham crackers.

Place on Parchment Paper:
- Place the chocolate-dipped and topped banana pops back onto the parchment-lined tray.

Freeze Again:
- Freeze the banana pops for an additional 30 minutes to allow the chocolate to set.

Serve:
- Once the chocolate is completely set, your chocolate-dipped banana pops are ready to be served.

Enjoy:
- Enjoy these delicious and fun chocolate-dipped banana pops as a refreshing and sweet treat.

These chocolate-dipped banana pops are not only tasty but also customizable with various toppings, making them a great dessert for parties, gatherings, or a fun family activity.

Banana Pudding

Ingredients:

- 3/4 cup granulated sugar
- 1/3 cup all-purpose flour
- 1/4 teaspoon salt
- 3 large egg yolks
- 2 cups whole milk
- 1 teaspoon vanilla extract
- 3 ripe bananas, sliced
- 1 box (about 12 ounces) vanilla wafer cookies
- 2 cups whipped cream or whipped topping

Instructions:

Prepare Pudding Base:
- In a medium saucepan, whisk together sugar, flour, and salt.

Add Egg Yolks:
- In a separate bowl, whisk the egg yolks. Gradually whisk the egg yolks into the sugar mixture in the saucepan.

Stir in Milk:
- Gradually whisk in the milk until smooth.

Cook Pudding:
- Place the saucepan over medium heat and cook, stirring constantly, until the mixture thickens and comes to a boil. This will take about 8-10 minutes.

Remove from Heat:
- Once the pudding has thickened, remove the saucepan from heat.

Add Vanilla:
- Stir in the vanilla extract.

Cool Pudding:
- Allow the pudding to cool for a few minutes, stirring occasionally to prevent a skin from forming.

Layering:
- In a serving dish or individual cups, start by layering vanilla wafer cookies at the bottom.
- Add a layer of sliced bananas on top of the cookies.

- Pour a portion of the warm pudding over the banana layer.

Repeat Layers:
- Repeat the layering process until you run out of ingredients, finishing with a layer of pudding on top.

Chill:
- Cover the dish with plastic wrap, ensuring it touches the surface of the pudding to prevent a skin from forming. Refrigerate for at least 4 hours or overnight.

Serve:
- Just before serving, top the banana pudding with whipped cream or whipped topping.

Enjoy:
- Serve and enjoy this delicious and classic banana pudding!

This banana pudding is a comforting and crowd-pleasing dessert with its creamy texture and layers of flavor. It's a perfect treat for family gatherings or any special occasion.

Banana Foster

Ingredients:

- 4 ripe bananas, peeled and sliced
- 1/2 cup unsalted butter
- 1 cup brown sugar, packed
- 1/2 teaspoon ground cinnamon
- 1/4 cup banana liqueur
- 1/2 cup dark rum
- Vanilla ice cream for serving

Instructions:

Prepare Ingredients:
- Peel the ripe bananas and slice them into rounds.

Melt Butter and Sugar:
- In a large skillet over medium heat, melt the butter. Add brown sugar and cinnamon, stirring until the sugar is dissolved.

Cook Bananas:
- Add the sliced bananas to the skillet and cook for 2-3 minutes, gently stirring to coat the bananas with the sugar mixture.

Add Liquor:
- Carefully add the banana liqueur to the skillet. Be cautious, as it may create flames when ignited.

Flambé (Optional):
- If you want to flambé the dish, carefully ignite the alcohol with a long lighter. Allow the flames to subside naturally or cover the skillet with a lid to extinguish them.

Add Rum:
- After the flames subside, add the dark rum to the skillet.

Flambé Again (Optional):
- Again, if you desire, carefully ignite the rum. Allow the flames to subside.

Serve:
- Spoon the bananas and sauce over vanilla ice cream.

Enjoy:
- Serve Banana Foster immediately and enjoy the delightful combination of warm, caramelized bananas over cool vanilla ice cream.

Note:

- Be cautious when working with open flames. If you're not comfortable flambéing, you can omit this step, and the dessert will still be delicious.
- Ensure that you're working in a well-ventilated area and keep a lid nearby to cover the skillet if needed.

Bananas Foster is a show-stopping dessert with a delightful combination of rich flavors. It's often served over vanilla ice cream, creating a perfect contrast of warm and cold, and it's sure to impress your guests.

Banana Tiramisu

Ingredients:

For the Tiramisu:

- 4 ripe bananas, peeled and sliced
- 1 cup strong brewed coffee, cooled
- 1/4 cup coffee liqueur (optional)
- 3 large eggs, separated
- 3/4 cup granulated sugar
- 1 cup mascarpone cheese
- 1 cup heavy cream
- 1 teaspoon vanilla extract
- Cocoa powder for dusting

For Assembly:

- Ladyfingers (optional)

Instructions:

Brew Coffee:
- Brew a strong cup of coffee and let it cool. If using coffee liqueur, mix it with the brewed coffee.

Prepare Bananas:
- Peel and slice the ripe bananas.

Make Mascarpone Mixture:
- In a bowl, whisk together egg yolks and sugar until pale and creamy.
- Add the mascarpone cheese and mix until smooth.

Whip Cream:
- In a separate bowl, whip the heavy cream until stiff peaks form.

Combine Mascarpone and Whipped Cream:
- Gently fold the whipped cream into the mascarpone mixture until well combined.

Beat Egg Whites:
- In another clean, dry bowl, whip the egg whites until stiff peaks form.

Fold Egg Whites:
- Carefully fold the whipped egg whites into the mascarpone mixture, ensuring a light and airy texture.

Assemble Tiramisu:
- In a serving dish or individual glasses, begin layering with a portion of the mascarpone mixture.
- Dip banana slices into the coffee mixture (and coffee liqueur if using) and arrange them over the mascarpone layer.
- Repeat the layers until you reach the top, finishing with a layer of mascarpone.

Chill:
- Cover the tiramisu and refrigerate for at least 4 hours or overnight to allow the flavors to meld.

Dust with Cocoa:
- Just before serving, dust the top of the Banana Tiramisu with cocoa powder.

Serve:
- Serve chilled, and enjoy this delightful Banana Tiramisu!

Optional:

- If you prefer the traditional ladyfinger layer, you can dip ladyfingers in the coffee mixture and layer them along with the bananas and mascarpone mixture.

This Banana Tiramisu offers a fruity and luscious variation of the classic dessert. The combination of creamy mascarpone, ripe bananas, and coffee creates a delightful flavor profile.

Banana Ice Cream

Ingredients:

- 4-5 ripe bananas, peeled and sliced into coins
- 1-2 tablespoons lemon juice (optional, to prevent browning)
- 1 teaspoon vanilla extract (optional)
- Pinch of salt (optional)

Instructions:

Prepare Bananas:
- Peel the ripe bananas and cut them into coins. If desired, toss the banana slices with lemon juice to prevent browning.

Freeze Bananas:
- Place the banana slices in a single layer on a parchment paper-lined tray or plate. Freeze for at least 2-3 hours or until solid.

Blend:
- Once the banana slices are frozen, transfer them to a blender or food processor. Add vanilla extract and a pinch of salt if using.

Blend until Creamy:
- Blend the frozen banana slices until smooth and creamy. You may need to stop and scrape down the sides of the blender or food processor a few times.

Adjust Consistency:
- If the banana ice cream is too thick, you can add a small amount of milk (dairy or plant-based) to achieve your desired consistency.

Optional Add-ins:
- Get creative with optional add-ins such as chocolate chips, chopped nuts, or a swirl of peanut butter. Add them during the blending process.

Serve Immediately or Freeze:
- Serve the banana ice cream immediately for a soft-serve texture. If you prefer a firmer texture, transfer it to a container and freeze for an additional 1-2 hours.

Enjoy:
- Scoop into bowls or cones and enjoy your homemade banana ice cream!

This banana ice cream is not only delicious but also a healthy and naturally sweet treat. It's a great way to use ripe bananas and enjoy a guilt-free dessert. Feel free to experiment with flavors and toppings to create your favorite variations.

Banana Cheesecake

Ingredients:

For the Crust:

- 1 1/2 cups graham cracker crumbs
- 1/3 cup melted butter
- 2 tablespoons granulated sugar

For the Cheesecake Filling:

- 4 ripe bananas, mashed
- 4 packages (8 ounces each) cream cheese, softened
- 1 1/2 cups granulated sugar
- 4 large eggs
- 1 teaspoon vanilla extract
- 1/4 cup all-purpose flour
- 1/2 cup sour cream

For the Banana Topping:

- 2 ripe bananas, sliced
- Lemon juice (to prevent browning)

Instructions:

Preheat the Oven:
- Preheat your oven to 325°F (163°C). Grease a 9-inch springform pan with butter or non-stick cooking spray.

Make the Crust:
- In a bowl, combine graham cracker crumbs, melted butter, and sugar. Press the mixture into the bottom of the prepared springform pan to form an even crust.

Bake the Crust:
- Bake the crust in the preheated oven for about 10 minutes. Remove from the oven and let it cool while you prepare the cheesecake filling.

Prepare Banana Topping:
- Slice 2 ripe bananas and toss the slices with a little lemon juice to prevent browning. Set aside for later.

Make the Cheesecake Filling:
- In a large mixing bowl, beat the softened cream cheese until smooth.
- Add mashed bananas, sugar, eggs, and vanilla extract. Mix until well combined.
- Gradually add the flour and sour cream, mixing until the batter is smooth and creamy.

Pour into Crust:
- Pour the banana cheesecake filling over the prepared crust.

Bake the Cheesecake:
- Bake in the preheated oven for about 1 hour or until the center is set and the top is golden brown.

Cool and Chill:
- Allow the cheesecake to cool in the oven with the door ajar for about 1 hour. Then, transfer it to the refrigerator and chill for at least 4 hours or overnight.

Add Banana Topping:
- Before serving, arrange the banana slices on top of the chilled cheesecake.

Slice and Serve:
- Slice the banana cheesecake and serve chilled. Optionally, you can garnish with additional whipped cream or a drizzle of caramel sauce.

Enjoy:
- Enjoy your delicious homemade banana cheesecake!

This banana cheesecake offers a wonderful combination of creamy cheesecake with the sweet and fruity flavor of ripe bananas. It's a perfect dessert for banana lovers and a delightful treat for any occasion.

Banana Fritters

Ingredients:

- 3 ripe bananas
- 1 cup all-purpose flour
- 2 tablespoons granulated sugar
- 1 teaspoon baking powder
- 1/4 teaspoon salt
- 1/2 teaspoon ground cinnamon (optional)
- 1/2 cup milk
- 1 large egg
- 1 teaspoon vanilla extract
- Oil for deep-frying
- Powdered sugar for dusting (optional)

Instructions:

Prepare Bananas:
- Peel the ripe bananas and slice them into rounds, approximately 1/2 inch thick.

Make Batter:
- In a mixing bowl, whisk together flour, sugar, baking powder, salt, and cinnamon if using.
- In a separate bowl, whisk together milk, egg, and vanilla extract.
- Pour the wet ingredients into the dry ingredients and stir until just combined. The batter should have a pancake-like consistency.

Heat Oil:
- In a deep pan or pot, heat oil to 350°F (175°C) for deep-frying.

Coat Bananas:
- Dip each banana slice into the batter, ensuring it's well coated.

Fry Banana Fritters:
- Carefully place the coated banana slices into the hot oil, a few at a time, to avoid overcrowding the pan.
- Fry the banana fritters for 2-3 minutes per side or until they are golden brown and crispy.

Drain Excess Oil:

- Use a slotted spoon to remove the banana fritters from the oil and place them on a paper towel-lined plate to drain excess oil.

Repeat:
- Continue the process until all banana slices are coated and fried.

Dust with Powdered Sugar (Optional):
- If desired, dust the banana fritters with powdered sugar before serving.

Serve Warm:
- Serve the banana fritters warm and enjoy!

Banana fritters are a delightful snack or dessert, and they're best enjoyed fresh and warm. The crispy exterior and soft, sweet interior make them a favorite treat in many cultures. Feel free to customize the batter with your preferred spices or add-ins for extra flavor.

Drinks:

Banana Smoothie

Ingredients:

- 2 ripe bananas, peeled and sliced
- 1 cup plain or vanilla yogurt (Greek yogurt or regular yogurt)
- 1/2 cup milk (dairy or plant-based)
- 1 tablespoon honey or maple syrup (optional, depending on sweetness preference)
- 1/2 teaspoon vanilla extract (optional)
- Ice cubes (optional)

Instructions:

Prepare Bananas:
- Peel the ripe bananas and slice them into smaller pieces for easier blending.

Add Ingredients to Blender:
- Place the banana slices in a blender.
- Add the yogurt, milk, honey or maple syrup (if using), and vanilla extract (if using).

Blend:
- Blend the ingredients on high speed until smooth and creamy. If the smoothie is too thick, you can add more milk to reach your desired consistency.

Add Ice Cubes (Optional):
- If you prefer a colder and icier smoothie, you can add a handful of ice cubes and blend again until smooth.

Taste and Adjust:
- Taste the smoothie and adjust the sweetness or thickness according to your preference. You can add more honey, milk, or yogurt as needed.

Pour and Serve:
- Pour the banana smoothie into glasses.

Optional Garnish:
- Optionally, garnish with banana slices or a sprinkle of cinnamon.

Enjoy:
- Enjoy your delicious and creamy banana smoothie!

This basic banana smoothie recipe is versatile, and you can customize it by adding ingredients like frozen berries, spinach, chia seeds, or protein powder for additional flavor and nutrition. It's a quick and easy way to enjoy the natural sweetness of bananas in a refreshing drink.

Banana Milkshake

Ingredients:

- 2 ripe bananas, peeled and sliced
- 2 cups cold milk (dairy or plant-based)
- 2 cups vanilla ice cream
- 2 tablespoons honey or sugar (optional, depending on sweetness preference)
- 1/2 teaspoon vanilla extract (optional)
- Ice cubes (optional)

Instructions:

Prepare Bananas:
- Peel the ripe bananas and slice them into smaller pieces for easier blending.

Add Ingredients to Blender:
- Place the banana slices in a blender.
- Add the cold milk, vanilla ice cream, honey or sugar (if using), and vanilla extract (if using).

Blend:
- Blend the ingredients on high speed until smooth and creamy. If the milkshake is too thick, you can add more milk to reach your desired consistency.

Add Ice Cubes (Optional):
- If you prefer a colder and icier milkshake, you can add a handful of ice cubes and blend again until smooth.

Taste and Adjust:
- Taste the milkshake and adjust the sweetness or thickness according to your preference. You can add more honey, sugar, or milk as needed.

Pour and Serve:
- Pour the banana milkshake into glasses.

Optional Garnish:
- Optionally, garnish with a swirl of whipped cream, a sprinkle of cinnamon, or a banana slice on the rim of the glass.

Enjoy:
- Enjoy your delicious and creamy banana milkshake!

Feel free to get creative and customize your banana milkshake by adding chocolate syrup, a dash of cinnamon, or a handful of nuts for extra flavor. It's a timeless and satisfying beverage that's perfect for a quick snack or a refreshing treat on a warm day.

Banana Berry Smoothie

Ingredients:

- 1 ripe banana, peeled and sliced
- 1 cup mixed berries (strawberries, blueberries, raspberries, blackberries)
- 1/2 cup yogurt (Greek yogurt or regular yogurt)
- 1/2 cup milk (dairy or plant-based)
- 1 tablespoon honey or maple syrup (optional, depending on sweetness preference)
- Ice cubes (optional)

Instructions:

Prepare Ingredients:
- Peel and slice the ripe banana.

Add Ingredients to Blender:
- Place the banana slices and mixed berries in a blender.
- Add yogurt, milk, and honey or maple syrup (if using).

Blend:
- Blend the ingredients on high speed until smooth and well combined. If the smoothie is too thick, you can add more milk to achieve your desired consistency.

Add Ice Cubes (Optional):
- If you prefer a colder and icier smoothie, you can add a handful of ice cubes and blend again until smooth.

Taste and Adjust:
- Taste the smoothie and adjust the sweetness or thickness according to your preference. You can add more honey, yogurt, or milk as needed.

Pour and Serve:
- Pour the Banana Berry Smoothie into glasses.

Optional Garnish:
- Optionally, garnish with a few whole berries on top.

Enjoy:
- Enjoy your refreshing and fruity Banana Berry Smoothie!

This smoothie is not only tasty but also packed with vitamins and antioxidants from the mixed berries. Feel free to customize by adding a handful of spinach or kale for a boost of greens, or include chia seeds or flaxseeds for added nutrition. It's a versatile and healthy beverage that's perfect for a quick breakfast or a refreshing snack.

Banana Coffee Smoothie

Ingredients:

- 1 ripe banana, peeled and sliced
- 1 cup strong brewed coffee, cooled
- 1/2 cup milk (dairy or plant-based)
- 1/2 cup plain or vanilla yogurt
- 1-2 tablespoons honey or maple syrup (optional, depending on sweetness preference)
- 1/2 teaspoon vanilla extract (optional)
- Ice cubes (optional)

Instructions:

Prepare Ingredients:
- Peel and slice the ripe banana.

Brew Coffee:
- Brew a cup of strong coffee and let it cool to room temperature or refrigerate it for a quicker cool down.

Add Ingredients to Blender:
- Place the banana slices in a blender.
- Add the cooled brewed coffee, milk, yogurt, honey or maple syrup (if using), and vanilla extract (if using).

Blend:
- Blend the ingredients on high speed until smooth and well combined. If you prefer a colder and icier smoothie, you can add a handful of ice cubes and blend again until smooth.

Taste and Adjust:
- Taste the smoothie and adjust the sweetness or thickness according to your preference. Add more honey, coffee, or milk as needed.

Pour and Serve:
- Pour the Banana Coffee Smoothie into glasses.

Optional Garnish:
- Optionally, garnish with a sprinkle of ground cinnamon or a few coffee beans on top.

Enjoy:
- Enjoy your delicious and energizing Banana Coffee Smoothie!

This smoothie is a great way to combine the flavors of your morning coffee with the nutritional benefits of bananas. It's a quick and convenient option for a breakfast on the go or a pick-me-up during the day. Adjust the coffee strength and sweetness to suit your taste preferences.

Banana and Coconut Water Cooler

Ingredients:

- 2 ripe bananas, peeled and sliced
- 2 cups coconut water
- 1 tablespoon honey or maple syrup (optional, depending on sweetness preference)
- Ice cubes (optional)
- Fresh mint leaves for garnish (optional)

Instructions:

Prepare Ingredients:
- Peel and slice the ripe bananas.

Add Ingredients to Blender:
- Place the banana slices in a blender.
- Add the coconut water and honey or maple syrup (if using).

Blend:
- Blend the ingredients on high speed until smooth and well combined.

Strain (Optional):
- If you prefer a smoother texture, you can strain the mixture using a fine mesh sieve or cheesecloth to remove any pulp. This step is optional.

Chill (Optional):
- If you'd like a colder beverage, refrigerate the mixture for a short time.

Add Ice Cubes (Optional):
- Add ice cubes to the blender and blend again for an extra refreshing cooler.

Pour and Serve:
- Pour the Banana and Coconut Water Cooler into glasses.

Optional Garnish:
- Garnish with fresh mint leaves for an extra burst of freshness.

Enjoy:
- Enjoy your refreshing Banana and Coconut Water Cooler!

This cooler is not only delicious but also a great way to stay hydrated, thanks to the electrolytes in coconut water. It's a perfect beverage for hot days or as a healthy alternative to sugary drinks. Adjust the sweetness and consistency according to your taste preferences.

-

Banana Lassi

Ingredients:

- 2 ripe bananas, peeled and sliced
- 1 cup plain yogurt
- 1/2 cup milk (dairy or plant-based)
- 2 tablespoons honey or sugar (adjust to taste)
- 1/2 teaspoon ground cardamom
- 1/4 teaspoon ground cinnamon
- Ice cubes (optional)
- Chopped nuts for garnish (optional)

Instructions:

Prepare Ingredients:
- Peel and slice the ripe bananas.

Add Ingredients to Blender:
- Place the banana slices in a blender.
- Add the plain yogurt, milk, honey or sugar, ground cardamom, and ground cinnamon.

Blend:
- Blend the ingredients on high speed until smooth and well combined.

Add Ice Cubes (Optional):
- If you prefer a colder lassi, you can add a handful of ice cubes to the blender and blend again until smooth.

Taste and Adjust:
- Taste the Banana Lassi and adjust the sweetness or thickness according to your preference. Add more honey, sugar, or milk if needed.

Pour and Serve:
- Pour the Banana Lassi into glasses.

Optional Garnish:
- Garnish with a sprinkle of ground cinnamon or chopped nuts for added texture.

Enjoy:
- Enjoy your creamy and flavorful Banana Lassi!

Banana Lassi is a delicious variation of the traditional lassi, and it makes for a wonderful and refreshing drink, especially during warm weather. The combination of ripe bananas and aromatic spices creates a delightful and satisfying beverage. Adjust the spice levels and sweetness to suit your taste preferences.

Banana Mojito

Ingredients:

- 1 ripe banana
- 10 fresh mint leaves
- 1 tablespoon granulated sugar
- Juice of 1 lime
- 2 ounces white rum
- 1 cup ice cubes
- Club soda
- Sliced banana and mint sprig for garnish (optional)

Instructions:

Prepare Ingredients:
- Peel and slice the ripe banana.

Muddle Mint and Banana:
- In a cocktail shaker or a mixing glass, muddle the mint leaves, sliced banana, and sugar together to release the mint's flavor and incorporate the banana.

Add Lime Juice and Rum:
- Add the lime juice and white rum to the shaker.

Shake:
- Fill the shaker with ice cubes and shake the mixture well to chill the ingredients.

Strain into Glass:
- Strain the mixture into a highball glass filled with ice cubes.

Top with Club Soda:
- Top off the glass with club soda to your desired level, stirring gently to combine the ingredients.

Optional Garnish:
- Garnish with a slice of banana and a sprig of mint on the rim of the glass.

Enjoy:
- Enjoy your tropical and fruity Banana Mojito!

This Banana Mojito brings a delightful sweetness to the traditional Mojito cocktail, making it a perfect choice for those who enjoy a hint of tropical flavor. Adjust the sweetness and lime juice according to your taste preferences. Cheers!

Banana and Strawberry Lemonade

Ingredients:

- 1 cup strawberries, hulled and halved
- 2 ripe bananas, peeled and sliced
- 1 cup freshly squeezed lemon juice (about 4-6 lemons)
- 1/2 cup granulated sugar (adjust to taste)
- 4 cups cold water
- Ice cubes
- Lemon slices and strawberry slices for garnish (optional)
- Mint leaves for garnish (optional)

Instructions:

Prepare Ingredients:
- Hull and halve the strawberries.
- Peel and slice the ripe bananas.
- Squeeze lemons to get 1 cup of fresh lemon juice.

Blend Fruit:
- In a blender, combine the strawberries, sliced bananas, and fresh lemon juice.

Blend Until Smooth:
- Blend the mixture until smooth and well combined.

Strain (Optional):
- If you prefer a smoother lemonade, you can strain the fruit puree using a fine mesh sieve or cheesecloth to remove any pulp. This step is optional.

Prepare Simple Syrup:
- In a small saucepan, heat 1/2 cup of water and dissolve the granulated sugar to make a simple syrup. Allow it to cool.

Mix Lemonade:
- In a large pitcher, combine the fruit puree, simple syrup, and cold water. Stir well to mix.

Adjust Sweetness:
- Taste the lemonade and adjust the sweetness by adding more sugar if needed.

Chill:

- Refrigerate the lemonade for at least 1-2 hours to chill and allow the flavors to meld.

Serve Over Ice:
- When ready to serve, pour the Banana and Strawberry Lemonade over ice cubes in glasses.

Optional Garnish:
- Garnish with lemon slices, strawberry slices, and mint leaves if desired.

Stir and Enjoy:
- Give it a gentle stir and enjoy your refreshing Banana and Strawberry Lemonade!

This fruity lemonade is perfect for warm days or as a delightful beverage for gatherings. It's a fantastic way to enjoy the combination of sweet bananas and juicy strawberries in a classic lemonade. Adjust the ingredients to suit your taste preferences.

Banana Colada

Ingredients:

- 1 ripe banana
- 1 cup pineapple chunks (fresh or canned)
- 2 ounces coconut cream
- 2 ounces white rum
- 1 cup ice cubes
- Pineapple slice and banana slice for garnish (optional)
- Maraschino cherry for garnish (optional)

Instructions:

Prepare Ingredients:
- Peel the ripe banana and break it into chunks.
- If using fresh pineapple, cut it into chunks. If using canned pineapple, drain the chunks.

Add Ingredients to Blender:
- In a blender, combine the ripe banana chunks, pineapple chunks, coconut cream, white rum, and ice cubes.

Blend Until Smooth:
- Blend the ingredients on high speed until smooth and creamy.

Check Consistency:
- Check the consistency of the Banana Colada. If it's too thick, you can add more ice cubes and blend again until desired consistency is reached.

Pour into Glass:
- Pour the Banana Colada into a chilled glass.

Optional Garnish:
- Garnish with a slice of pineapple and a slice of banana on the rim of the glass. Add a maraschino cherry on top for an extra tropical touch.

Enjoy:
- Enjoy your delicious and tropical Banana Colada!

This Banana Colada offers a delightful blend of sweet bananas, creamy coconut, and tropical pineapple, making it a perfect cocktail for beachy vibes or summer gatherings. Adjust the rum and sweetness according to your taste preferences. Cheers!

Banana Iced Tea

Ingredients:

- 3 ripe bananas
- 4 cups water
- 4 tea bags (black tea or your preferred variety)
- 1/4 cup honey or sugar (adjust to taste)
- Ice cubes
- Lemon slices or mint leaves for garnish (optional)

Instructions:

Prepare Ingredients:
- Peel the ripe bananas and slice them.

Make Banana Infusion:
- In a saucepan, combine the sliced bananas and water. Bring the mixture to a boil.
- Once boiling, reduce the heat and simmer for about 10-15 minutes, allowing the bananas to infuse into the water.

Strain Banana Infusion:
- After simmering, strain the banana-infused water to remove the banana pieces, resulting in banana-infused water.

Brew Tea:
- In the banana-infused water, steep the tea bags according to the package instructions.

Sweeten:
- While the tea is still warm, add honey or sugar to sweeten the Banana Iced Tea. Adjust the sweetness according to your taste.

Chill:
- Allow the sweetened tea to cool to room temperature and then refrigerate until chilled.

Serve Over Ice:
- Pour the chilled Banana Iced Tea over ice cubes in glasses.

Optional Garnish:
- Garnish with lemon slices or mint leaves if desired.

Stir and Enjoy:
- Give it a gentle stir and enjoy your unique and fruity Banana Iced Tea!

This Banana Iced Tea offers a refreshing and tropical flavor that's perfect for warm days or as a special beverage for gatherings. Feel free to experiment with the sweetness level and add any additional garnishes you prefer.

Breads and Pastries:

Banana Zucchini Bread

Ingredients:

- 2 ripe bananas, mashed
- 1 cup grated zucchini, excess moisture squeezed out
- 1/2 cup unsalted butter, melted
- 1 teaspoon vanilla extract
- 1/2 cup granulated sugar
- 1/2 cup brown sugar, packed
- 2 large eggs
- 2 cups all-purpose flour
- 1 teaspoon baking powder
- 1/2 teaspoon baking soda
- 1/2 teaspoon salt
- 1 teaspoon ground cinnamon
- 1/2 teaspoon ground nutmeg
- 1/2 cup chopped nuts (optional)
- 1/2 cup chocolate chips (optional)

Instructions:

Preheat Oven:
- Preheat your oven to 350°F (175°C). Grease and flour a 9x5-inch loaf pan.

Prepare Zucchini:
- Grate the zucchini and use a clean kitchen towel or paper towels to squeeze out excess moisture.

Mix Wet Ingredients:
- In a large mixing bowl, combine the mashed bananas, grated zucchini, melted butter, vanilla extract, granulated sugar, brown sugar, and eggs. Mix until well combined.

Combine Dry Ingredients:
- In a separate bowl, whisk together the flour, baking powder, baking soda, salt, ground cinnamon, and ground nutmeg.

Combine Wet and Dry Ingredients:

- Add the dry ingredients to the wet ingredients and stir until just combined. Be careful not to overmix.

Add Nuts or Chocolate Chips (Optional):
- If using, fold in chopped nuts or chocolate chips into the batter.

Pour into Pan:
- Pour the batter into the prepared loaf pan, spreading it evenly.

Bake:
- Bake in the preheated oven for 55-65 minutes or until a toothpick inserted into the center comes out clean or with a few moist crumbs.

Cool:
- Allow the Banana Zucchini Bread to cool in the pan for about 10 minutes, then transfer it to a wire rack to cool completely.

Slice and Serve:
- Once cooled, slice the bread and serve. Enjoy!

This Banana Zucchini Bread is a wonderful way to use up overripe bananas and adds a subtle hint of vegetables with the zucchini. The addition of nuts or chocolate chips is optional but adds extra texture and flavor. It's a delightful treat for breakfast or as a snack.

Banana Blueberry Muffins

Ingredients:

- 1 1/2 cups all-purpose flour
- 1 teaspoon baking powder
- 1/2 teaspoon baking soda
- 1/4 teaspoon salt
- 1/2 teaspoon ground cinnamon
- 2 ripe bananas, mashed
- 1/2 cup granulated sugar
- 1/4 cup unsalted butter, melted
- 1 large egg
- 1 teaspoon vanilla extract
- 1 cup fresh or frozen blueberries
- Optional: Turbinado sugar for sprinkling on top

Instructions:

Preheat Oven:
- Preheat your oven to 375°F (190°C). Line a muffin tin with paper liners or grease the cups.

Combine Dry Ingredients:
- In a medium bowl, whisk together the flour, baking powder, baking soda, salt, and ground cinnamon. Set aside.

Mix Wet Ingredients:
- In a large bowl, mash the ripe bananas. Add the granulated sugar, melted butter, egg, and vanilla extract. Mix until well combined.

Combine Wet and Dry Ingredients:
- Add the dry ingredients to the wet ingredients and stir until just combined. Be careful not to overmix.

Fold in Blueberries:
- Gently fold in the blueberries into the batter. If using frozen blueberries, toss them in a bit of flour before folding them in to prevent them from sinking to the bottom.

Fill Muffin Cups:
- Spoon the batter into the prepared muffin cups, filling each about 2/3 full.

Optional Topping:

- If desired, sprinkle the tops of the muffins with a bit of Turbinado sugar for a crunchy topping.

Bake:
- Bake in the preheated oven for 18-22 minutes, or until a toothpick inserted into the center comes out clean or with a few moist crumbs.

Cool:
- Allow the Banana Blueberry Muffins to cool in the muffin tin for a few minutes, then transfer them to a wire rack to cool completely.

Enjoy:
- Once cooled, enjoy your delicious Banana Blueberry Muffins!

These muffins are perfect for breakfast, brunch, or as a snack. The combination of ripe bananas and juicy blueberries creates a delightful flavor profile. Feel free to customize the recipe by adding nuts or a streusel topping if desired.

Banana Chocolate Chip Scones

Ingredients:

- 2 cups all-purpose flour
- 1/4 cup granulated sugar
- 1 tablespoon baking powder
- 1/2 teaspoon salt
- 1/2 cup unsalted butter, cold and cubed
- 1/2 cup mashed ripe bananas (about 2 medium-sized bananas)
- 1/2 cup milk (dairy or plant-based)
- 1 teaspoon vanilla extract
- 1/2 cup chocolate chips (dark or semi-sweet)
- Optional: Additional sugar for sprinkling on top

Instructions:

Preheat Oven:
- Preheat your oven to 425°F (220°C). Line a baking sheet with parchment paper or lightly grease it.

Combine Dry Ingredients:
- In a large bowl, whisk together the flour, sugar, baking powder, and salt.

Cut in Butter:
- Add the cold, cubed butter to the dry ingredients. Using a pastry cutter or your fingers, work the butter into the flour until the mixture resembles coarse crumbs.

Mix Wet Ingredients:
- In a separate bowl, mix together the mashed bananas, milk, and vanilla extract.

Combine Wet and Dry Ingredients:
- Add the wet ingredients to the dry ingredients and stir until just combined.

Fold in Chocolate Chips:
- Gently fold in the chocolate chips into the dough.

Shape the Dough:
- Turn the dough out onto a lightly floured surface. Pat it into a circle about 1-inch (2.5 cm) thick.

Cut Scones:

- Using a sharp knife or a biscuit cutter, cut the dough into wedges or rounds.

Place on Baking Sheet:
- Place the shaped scones onto the prepared baking sheet, leaving some space between each.

Optional Sugar Topping:
- If desired, sprinkle the tops of the scones with a bit of sugar for a sweet crunch.

Bake:
- Bake in the preheated oven for 12-15 minutes or until the edges are golden brown.

Cool:
- Allow the Banana Chocolate Chip Scones to cool on the baking sheet for a few minutes, then transfer them to a wire rack to cool completely.

Enjoy:
- Once cooled, enjoy your delicious Banana Chocolate Chip Scones with a cup of tea or coffee!

These scones are a wonderful treat for breakfast or afternoon tea. The combination of banana and chocolate creates a delightful flavor, and the scones have a tender, flaky texture.

Banana Cinnamon Rolls

Ingredients:

For the Dough:

- 1 cup mashed ripe bananas (about 2-3 medium bananas)
- 1/2 cup warm milk
- 2 1/4 teaspoons active dry yeast (1 packet)
- 1/4 cup granulated sugar
- 1/4 cup unsalted butter, melted
- 1 teaspoon vanilla extract
- 1/2 teaspoon salt
- 3 to 3 1/2 cups all-purpose flour

For the Filling:

- 1/2 cup unsalted butter, softened
- 1 cup brown sugar, packed
- 2 teaspoons ground cinnamon
- 1/2 cup chopped nuts (optional)
- 1/2 cup raisins or currants (optional)

For the Cream Cheese Frosting:

- 4 ounces cream cheese, softened
- 1/4 cup unsalted butter, softened
- 1 cup powdered sugar
- 1/2 teaspoon vanilla extract

Instructions:

For the Dough:

    Activate Yeast:
- In a bowl, combine warm milk and yeast. Let it sit for about 5 minutes until the yeast is activated and becomes frothy.

Mix Ingredients:
- In a large bowl, mix mashed bananas, melted butter, sugar, vanilla extract, and salt. Add the activated yeast mixture and stir to combine.

Add Flour:
- Gradually add 3 cups of all-purpose flour, one cup at a time, stirring well after each addition. Continue adding flour until the dough comes together.

Knead Dough:
- Turn the dough onto a floured surface and knead for about 5-7 minutes until it becomes smooth and elastic. Add more flour if needed.

Rise Dough:
- Place the dough in a greased bowl, cover it with a damp cloth, and let it rise in a warm place for about 1-2 hours, or until it doubles in size.

For the Filling:

Prepare Filling:
- In a bowl, mix softened butter, brown sugar, cinnamon, chopped nuts (if using), and raisins or currants (if using).

Assembly and Baking:

Roll Out Dough:
- Punch down the risen dough and roll it out on a floured surface into a large rectangle.

Spread Filling:
- Spread the prepared filling evenly over the dough.

Roll Dough:
- Starting from one long edge, tightly roll the dough into a log.

Cut Rolls:
- Using a sharp knife or dental floss, cut the rolled dough into 12-15 slices.

Place in Pan:
- Place the sliced rolls in a greased baking pan, leaving a little space between each.

Rise Again:
- Cover the rolls with a damp cloth and let them rise for another 30-45 minutes.

Bake:

- Preheat the oven to 350°F (175°C). Bake the rolls for 20-25 minutes or until they are golden brown.

For the Cream Cheese Frosting:

Prepare Frosting:
- In a bowl, beat together softened cream cheese, softened butter, powdered sugar, and vanilla extract until smooth.

Frost Rolls:
- Once the rolls have cooled slightly, spread the cream cheese frosting over the top.

Serve and Enjoy:
- Serve the Banana Cinnamon Rolls warm and enjoy!

These Banana Cinnamon Rolls are a delightful treat with a fruity twist. The cream cheese frosting adds a perfect touch of sweetness to these soft and flavorful rolls.

Enjoy them for breakfast or as a delicious dessert!

Banana Cranberry Bread

Ingredients:

- 2 to 3 ripe bananas, mashed
- 1/2 cup unsalted butter, melted
- 1 teaspoon vanilla extract
- 1/2 cup granulated sugar
- 1/2 cup brown sugar, packed
- 2 large eggs
- 2 cups all-purpose flour
- 1 teaspoon baking powder
- 1/2 teaspoon baking soda
- 1/2 teaspoon salt
- 1 cup fresh or frozen cranberries
- 1/2 cup chopped nuts (walnuts or pecans), optional

Instructions:

Preheat Oven:
- Preheat your oven to 350°F (175°C). Grease and flour a 9x5-inch loaf pan.

Prepare Ingredients:
- Mash the ripe bananas with a fork.

Mix Wet Ingredients:
- In a large mixing bowl, combine the mashed bananas, melted butter, vanilla extract, granulated sugar, and brown sugar. Mix until well combined.

Add Eggs:
- Add the eggs to the wet ingredients one at a time, mixing well after each addition.

Combine Dry Ingredients:
- In a separate bowl, whisk together the flour, baking powder, baking soda, and salt.

Add Dry Ingredients:
- Gradually add the dry ingredients to the wet ingredients, stirring until just combined. Be careful not to overmix.

Fold in Cranberries and Nuts:
- Gently fold in the cranberries and chopped nuts (if using) into the batter.

Pour into Pan:
- Pour the batter into the prepared loaf pan, spreading it evenly.

Bake:
- Bake in the preheated oven for 60-70 minutes or until a toothpick inserted into the center comes out clean or with a few moist crumbs.

Cool:
- Allow the Banana Cranberry Bread to cool in the pan for about 10 minutes, then transfer it to a wire rack to cool completely.

Slice and Serve:
- Once cooled, slice the bread and serve. Enjoy!

This Banana Cranberry Bread is perfect for the holiday season or any time you want a slightly tart and fruity twist to your banana bread. The combination of sweet bananas and tart cranberries creates a delicious flavor profile. Adjust the sweetness and add nuts for extra texture if desired.

Banana Nut Bread Pudding

Ingredients:

For the Banana Nut Bread:

- 2 to 3 ripe bananas, mashed
- 1/2 cup unsalted butter, melted
- 1 teaspoon vanilla extract
- 1/2 cup granulated sugar
- 1/2 cup brown sugar, packed
- 2 large eggs
- 2 cups all-purpose flour
- 1 teaspoon baking powder
- 1/2 teaspoon baking soda
- 1/2 teaspoon salt
- 1/2 cup chopped nuts (walnuts or pecans)

For the Bread Pudding:

- 1 loaf of day-old banana nut bread, cut into cubes
- 2 cups milk
- 1 cup heavy cream
- 3/4 cup granulated sugar
- 4 large eggs
- 1 teaspoon vanilla extract
- 1/2 teaspoon ground cinnamon
- 1/4 teaspoon salt
- 1/2 cup chopped nuts (walnuts or pecans)

Instructions:

For the Banana Nut Bread:

 Preheat Oven:
  - Preheat your oven to 350°F (175°C). Grease and flour a loaf pan.
 Prepare Banana Nut Bread Batter:

- In a large mixing bowl, combine mashed bananas, melted butter, vanilla extract, granulated sugar, and brown sugar. Mix until well combined.

Add Eggs:
- Add the eggs to the banana mixture one at a time, mixing well after each addition.

Combine Dry Ingredients:
- In a separate bowl, whisk together the flour, baking powder, baking soda, and salt.

Mix Dry Ingredients:
- Gradually add the dry ingredients to the wet ingredients, stirring until just combined. Fold in the chopped nuts.

Bake Banana Nut Bread:
- Pour the batter into the prepared loaf pan and bake in the preheated oven for 55-65 minutes or until a toothpick inserted into the center comes out clean or with a few moist crumbs.

Cool Banana Nut Bread:
- Allow the banana nut bread to cool in the pan for about 10 minutes, then transfer it to a wire rack to cool completely.

For the Bread Pudding:

Preheat Oven:
- Preheat your oven to 350°F (175°C).

Cut Bread into Cubes:
- Cut the day-old banana nut bread into bite-sized cubes.

Prepare Custard Mixture:
- In a bowl, whisk together milk, heavy cream, granulated sugar, eggs, vanilla extract, ground cinnamon, and salt until well combined.

Assemble Bread Pudding:
- Place the banana nut bread cubes in a greased baking dish. Pour the custard mixture over the bread cubes, ensuring they are well-coated. Let it sit for about 15-20 minutes to allow the bread to absorb the custard.

Add Chopped Nuts:
- Sprinkle chopped nuts over the top of the bread pudding.

Bake Bread Pudding:
- Bake in the preheated oven for 45-50 minutes or until the top is golden brown and the custard is set.

Cool Slightly:

- Allow the banana nut bread pudding to cool slightly before serving.

Serve:
- Serve warm, and optionally, drizzle with caramel sauce or a scoop of vanilla ice cream.

Enjoy your delicious Banana Nut Bread Pudding, a comforting and flavorful dessert that combines the best of banana bread and bread pudding!

Banana Date Muffins

Ingredients:

- 2 to 3 ripe bananas, mashed
- 1/2 cup unsalted butter, melted (or substitute with melted coconut oil for a dairy-free version)
- 1/2 cup pure maple syrup or honey
- 1 large egg
- 1 teaspoon vanilla extract
- 1 1/2 cups all-purpose flour
- 1 teaspoon baking powder
- 1/2 teaspoon baking soda
- 1/2 teaspoon salt
- 1 teaspoon ground cinnamon
- 1/2 cup chopped dates
- 1/2 cup chopped nuts (optional, such as walnuts or pecans)

Instructions:

Preheat Oven:
- Preheat your oven to 350°F (175°C). Line a muffin tin with paper liners or grease the cups.

Mix Wet Ingredients:
- In a large bowl, combine mashed bananas, melted butter (or oil), maple syrup (or honey), egg, and vanilla extract. Mix until well combined.

Combine Dry Ingredients:
- In a separate bowl, whisk together the flour, baking powder, baking soda, salt, and ground cinnamon.

Add Dry Ingredients:
- Gradually add the dry ingredients to the wet ingredients, stirring until just combined. Be careful not to overmix.

Fold in Dates and Nuts:
- Gently fold in the chopped dates and nuts (if using) into the batter.

Fill Muffin Cups:
- Spoon the batter into the prepared muffin cups, filling each about 2/3 full.

Bake:

- Bake in the preheated oven for 18-22 minutes or until a toothpick inserted into the center comes out clean or with a few moist crumbs.

Cool:
- Allow the Banana Date Muffins to cool in the muffin tin for a few minutes, then transfer them to a wire rack to cool completely.

Serve:
- Once cooled, serve and enjoy your delicious and naturally sweetened Banana Date Muffins!

These muffins are perfect for breakfast, brunch, or as a snack. The combination of ripe bananas and sweet dates creates a wonderful flavor, and the optional addition of nuts adds a delightful crunch. Adjust the sweetness and add-ins according to your taste preferences.

Banana Cream Cheese Danish

Ingredients:

For the Danish Dough:

- 1 sheet puff pastry (thawed if frozen)

For the Banana Cream Cheese Filling:

- 1/2 cup ripe bananas, mashed
- 4 ounces cream cheese, softened
- 1/4 cup granulated sugar
- 1 teaspoon vanilla extract
- 1 tablespoon all-purpose flour

For the Glaze:

- 1/2 cup powdered sugar
- 1-2 tablespoons milk
- 1/2 teaspoon vanilla extract

Instructions:

Preheat Oven:
- Preheat your oven to 400°F (200°C). Line a baking sheet with parchment paper.

Prepare Banana Cream Cheese Filling:
- In a bowl, combine mashed bananas, softened cream cheese, granulated sugar, vanilla extract, and flour. Mix until well combined.

Roll Out Puff Pastry:
- On a lightly floured surface, roll out the puff pastry sheet into a rectangle.

Cut Pastry:
- Cut the pastry into squares or rectangles, depending on your preference.

Add Filling:
- Spoon a dollop of the banana cream cheese filling onto the center of each pastry square.

Fold Pastry:
- Fold the edges of the pastry over the filling, creating a border.

Bake:
- Place the filled pastries on the prepared baking sheet and bake in the preheated oven for 15-20 minutes or until golden brown and puffed.

Prepare Glaze:
- While the Danish is baking, prepare the glaze by whisking together powdered sugar, milk, and vanilla extract in a small bowl. Adjust the consistency by adding more milk if needed.

Glaze Danish:
- Once the Danish is out of the oven and slightly cooled, drizzle the glaze over the top.

Serve:
- Serve the Banana Cream Cheese Danish warm and enjoy!

This Banana Cream Cheese Danish is a delightful treat for breakfast, brunch, or as a dessert. The combination of creamy banana filling and flaky pastry creates a delicious pastry that is sure to be a hit. Customize it by adding a sprinkle of chopped nuts or a dusting of cinnamon if desired.

Banana Pecan Sticky Buns

Ingredients:

For the Dough:

- 1 package (2 1/4 teaspoons) active dry yeast
- 1 cup warm milk (about 110°F/43°C)
- 1/4 cup granulated sugar
- 1/3 cup unsalted butter, melted
- 1 teaspoon vanilla extract
- 1/2 teaspoon salt
- 3 1/2 to 4 cups all-purpose flour

For the Filling:

- 1/2 cup unsalted butter, softened
- 1 cup packed brown sugar
- 1 tablespoon ground cinnamon
- 2 ripe bananas, mashed
- 1 cup chopped pecans

For the Sticky Topping:

- 1/2 cup unsalted butter
- 1 cup packed brown sugar
- 1/4 cup light corn syrup
- 1 cup chopped pecans

Instructions:

For the Dough:

Activate Yeast:
- In a small bowl, dissolve the yeast in warm milk. Let it sit for about 5 minutes until the yeast is activated and becomes frothy.

Mix Ingredients:
- In a large mixing bowl, combine the activated yeast mixture, sugar, melted butter, vanilla extract, and salt. Gradually add the flour, one cup at a time, until a soft dough forms.

Knead Dough:
- Turn the dough onto a floured surface and knead for about 5-7 minutes until it becomes smooth and elastic. Add more flour if needed.

First Rise:
- Place the dough in a greased bowl, cover it with a damp cloth, and let it rise in a warm place for about 1 to 1.5 hours, or until it doubles in size.

For the Filling:

Mix Filling:
- In a bowl, mix together the softened butter, brown sugar, ground cinnamon, mashed bananas, and chopped pecans.

For the Sticky Topping:

Prepare Topping:
- In a saucepan, melt the butter over medium heat. Add the brown sugar and corn syrup, stirring until the sugar dissolves. Remove from heat and stir in the chopped pecans.

Assembly and Baking:

Preheat Oven:
- Preheat your oven to 350°F (175°C).

Roll Out Dough:
- Roll out the risen dough on a floured surface into a rectangle.

Spread Filling:
- Spread the banana and pecan filling evenly over the rolled-out dough.

Roll Dough:
- Starting from one long edge, tightly roll the dough into a log.

Cut Rolls:
- Using a sharp knife or dental floss, cut the rolled dough into 12-15 slices.

Prepare Baking Dish:
- In a greased baking dish, pour the prepared sticky topping.

Place Rolls in Dish:
- Place the sliced rolls in the prepared baking dish on top of the sticky topping.

Second Rise:

- Cover the baking dish with a damp cloth and let the rolls rise for another 30-45 minutes.

Bake:
- Bake in the preheated oven for 25-30 minutes or until the rolls are golden brown.

Cool Slightly:
- Allow the Banana Pecan Sticky Buns to cool slightly before inverting the baking dish onto a serving platter.

Serve:
- Serve the sticky buns warm, allowing the gooey topping to drip down the sides.

Enjoy your delicious and gooey Banana Pecan Sticky Buns! The combination of ripe bananas, pecans, and the sticky caramel topping creates a delightful treat perfect for breakfast or brunch.

Banana Streusel Coffee Cake

Ingredients:

For the Streusel Topping:

- 1/2 cup all-purpose flour
- 1/4 cup granulated sugar
- 1/4 cup brown sugar, packed
- 1/2 teaspoon ground cinnamon
- 1/4 cup unsalted butter, melted
- 1/2 cup chopped nuts (optional, such as walnuts or pecans)

For the Cake:

- 2 to 3 ripe bananas, mashed
- 1 teaspoon lemon juice (to prevent browning)
- 1/2 cup unsalted butter, softened
- 1 cup granulated sugar
- 2 large eggs
- 1 teaspoon vanilla extract
- 2 cups all-purpose flour
- 1 teaspoon baking powder
- 1/2 teaspoon baking soda
- 1/4 teaspoon salt
- 1 cup sour cream or plain yogurt

Instructions:

For the Streusel Topping:

Mix Streusel Ingredients:
- In a bowl, combine the flour, granulated sugar, brown sugar, ground cinnamon, melted butter, and chopped nuts (if using). Mix until the mixture resembles coarse crumbs. Set aside.

For the Cake:

Preheat Oven:

- Preheat your oven to 350°F (175°C). Grease and flour a 9x13-inch baking pan.

Prepare Streusel Cake Batter:
- Mash the ripe bananas and mix them with lemon juice to prevent browning.

Cream Butter and Sugar:
- In a large mixing bowl, cream together the softened butter and granulated sugar until light and fluffy.

Add Eggs and Vanilla:
- Add the eggs, one at a time, beating well after each addition. Add the vanilla extract and mix until combined.

Combine Dry Ingredients:
- In a separate bowl, whisk together the flour, baking powder, baking soda, and salt.

Alternate Additions:
- Gradually add the dry ingredients to the banana mixture, alternating with the sour cream or yogurt. Begin and end with the dry ingredients. Mix until just combined.

Layer Batter and Streusel:
- Spread half of the cake batter into the prepared baking pan. Sprinkle half of the streusel topping over the batter. Repeat with the remaining batter and streusel.

Swirl with a Knife:
- Use a knife to swirl the batter and streusel together gently.

Bake:
- Bake in the preheated oven for 40-45 minutes or until a toothpick inserted into the center comes out clean or with a few moist crumbs.

Cool:
- Allow the Banana Streusel Coffee Cake to cool in the pan for about 15 minutes, then transfer it to a wire rack to cool completely.

Slice and Serve:
- Once cooled, slice the coffee cake into squares and serve.

Enjoy your delicious Banana Streusel Coffee Cake! The combination of moist banana cake and the crunchy streusel topping makes this a perfect treat for breakfast, brunch, or dessert.

Breakfast and Brunch:

Grilled Banana and Chicken Skewers

Ingredients:

For the Marinade:

- 1.5 lbs boneless, skinless chicken breasts, cut into bite-sized cubes
- 2 ripe bananas, mashed
- 1/4 cup soy sauce
- 2 tablespoons honey
- 2 tablespoons olive oil
- 2 cloves garlic, minced
- 1 teaspoon ground ginger
- Salt and pepper to taste

For the Skewers:

- Wooden or metal skewers (if using wooden skewers, soak them in water for about 30 minutes to prevent burning)
- Sliced bananas (for grilling alongside chicken, optional)

Instructions:

Prepare Marinade:
- In a bowl, whisk together mashed bananas, soy sauce, honey, olive oil, minced garlic, ground ginger, salt, and pepper to create the marinade.

Marinate Chicken:
- Place the chicken cubes in a resealable plastic bag or shallow dish. Pour the marinade over the chicken, making sure it is well-coated. Seal the bag or cover the dish and refrigerate for at least 30 minutes to allow the flavors to meld.

Preheat Grill:
- Preheat your grill to medium-high heat.

Assemble Skewers:

- Thread the marinated chicken cubes onto the skewers, leaving a small space between each piece.

Grill Chicken Skewers:
- Place the chicken skewers on the preheated grill. Grill for about 10-15 minutes, turning occasionally, or until the chicken is fully cooked and has a nice char.

Optional: Grill Banana Slices:
- If you like, you can grill banana slices alongside the chicken skewers for a sweet and caramelized flavor. Simply place the banana slices on the grill for a few minutes on each side until they are lightly browned.

Serve:
- Once the chicken skewers are cooked through, remove them from the grill. Serve them with grilled banana slices if desired.

Garnish:
- Garnish the skewers with chopped fresh cilantro, green onions, or sesame seeds for added flavor and presentation.

Enjoy:
- Enjoy your Grilled Banana and Chicken Skewers as a tasty and unique dish!

These skewers offer a delightful combination of sweet and savory flavors, making them perfect for a summer barbecue or a unique twist on grilled chicken. Feel free to customize the recipe with your favorite herbs and spices for added depth of flavor.

Banana and Ham Breakfast Burrito

Ingredients:

- 1 large flour tortilla
- 2 eggs, scrambled
- 1 ripe banana, sliced
- 2 slices of ham, cooked
- 1/4 cup shredded cheddar cheese
- Salt and pepper to taste
- Optional: Salsa or hot sauce for serving

Instructions:

Cook Eggs:
- In a skillet, scramble the eggs over medium heat until they are fully cooked. Season with salt and pepper to taste.

Prepare Tortilla:
- Warm the flour tortilla in the skillet or microwave according to package instructions.

Assemble Burrito:
- Lay the warm tortilla on a flat surface. Place the scrambled eggs in the center of the tortilla.

Add Banana and Ham:
- Add sliced bananas and cooked ham slices on top of the eggs.

Sprinkle Cheese:
- Sprinkle shredded cheddar cheese over the filling.

Fold and Roll:
- Fold in the sides of the tortilla and then roll it up tightly, creating a burrito.

Serve:
- Place the burrito seam-side down on a plate. Optionally, you can cut it in half diagonally for easier handling.

Optional Toppings:
- Serve with salsa or hot sauce on the side if you'd like to add a bit of heat to your breakfast.

Enjoy:
- Enjoy your unique Banana and Ham Breakfast Burrito!

This combination may sound unusual, but the sweetness of the banana complements the savory flavors of the ham and eggs. It's a quick and easy breakfast option that provides a balance of protein and carbohydrates. Feel free to customize the recipe by adding other ingredients like cheese, avocado, or your favorite breakfast toppings.

Banana and Bacon Stuffed French Toast

Ingredients:

For the Stuffed French Toast:

- 8 slices of thick-cut bread (such as brioche or challah)
- 2 ripe bananas, sliced
- 8 slices of cooked bacon
- 4 ounces cream cheese, softened
- 4 large eggs
- 1 cup milk
- 1 teaspoon vanilla extract
- 1/2 teaspoon ground cinnamon
- Pinch of salt
- Butter for cooking

For Serving:

- Maple syrup
- Powdered sugar (optional)
- Sliced bananas and cooked bacon for garnish (optional)

Instructions:

Prepare the Filling:
- In a bowl, mix the softened cream cheese until smooth. Spread a generous layer of cream cheese on four slices of bread.

Add Banana and Bacon:
- On the cream cheese-covered slices, layer sliced bananas and cooked bacon. Top each with another slice of bread to form sandwiches.

Make the Egg Mixture:
- In a shallow dish, whisk together eggs, milk, vanilla extract, ground cinnamon, and a pinch of salt.

Dip and Coat:
- Dip each stuffed sandwich into the egg mixture, making sure both sides are well-coated.

Cook French Toast:

- In a skillet or griddle, melt butter over medium heat. Cook each stuffed French toast sandwich until golden brown on both sides, ensuring that the filling is heated through.

Serve:
- Place the stuffed French toast on serving plates. Drizzle with maple syrup and sprinkle with powdered sugar if desired.

Garnish:
- Garnish with additional sliced bananas and bacon if you like.

Enjoy:
- Serve immediately and enjoy your delicious Banana and Bacon Stuffed French Toast!

This breakfast dish combines the sweetness of bananas with the savory goodness of bacon, creating a flavorful and satisfying meal. It's perfect for a special brunch or when you want to treat yourself to something extra delicious.

Banana and Shrimp Lettuce Wraps

Ingredients:

For the Banana Shrimp Filling:

- 1 lb shrimp, peeled and deveined
- 2 ripe bananas, sliced
- 2 tablespoons olive oil
- 3 cloves garlic, minced
- 1 teaspoon ginger, grated
- 1 tablespoon soy sauce
- 1 tablespoon honey or maple syrup
- Salt and pepper to taste
- Fresh cilantro, chopped (for garnish)

For Lettuce Wraps:

- Large lettuce leaves (such as iceberg or butter lettuce)
- Optional toppings: sliced avocado, chopped tomatoes, shredded carrots

Instructions:

Prepare the Banana Shrimp Filling:
- In a large skillet or wok, heat olive oil over medium-high heat.

Cook Shrimp:
- Add shrimp to the skillet and cook until they turn pink and opaque, usually 2-3 minutes per side.

Add Garlic and Ginger:
- Add minced garlic and grated ginger to the skillet. Sauté for about 1 minute until fragrant.

Add Banana Slices:
- Add sliced bananas to the skillet and gently stir to combine with the shrimp, garlic, and ginger.

Make Sauce:
- In a small bowl, mix soy sauce and honey (or maple syrup). Pour the sauce over the shrimp and banana mixture. Stir to coat evenly. Cook for an

additional 1-2 minutes until the bananas are slightly caramelized and the sauce thickens.

Season:
- Season with salt and pepper to taste. Adjust the sweetness or saltiness according to your preference.

Garnish:
- Sprinkle fresh cilantro over the mixture for added flavor and freshness.

Prepare Lettuce Wraps:
- Arrange large lettuce leaves on a serving platter.

Assemble Wraps:
- Spoon the banana and shrimp mixture into each lettuce leaf. Optionally, add sliced avocado, chopped tomatoes, or shredded carrots on top for extra crunch and freshness.

Serve:
- Serve the Banana and Shrimp Lettuce Wraps immediately.

These lettuce wraps offer a delightful combination of flavors with the sweetness of ripe bananas and the savory taste of shrimp. They make for a light and refreshing meal, perfect for a healthy lunch or appetizer. Adjust the ingredients and seasonings to suit your taste preferences.

Banana and Quinoa Stuffed Peppers

Ingredients:

- 4 large bell peppers, halved and seeds removed
- 1 cup cooked quinoa
- 2 ripe bananas, diced
- 1 cup black beans, cooked and drained
- 1 cup corn kernels (fresh, frozen, or canned)
- 1 cup diced tomatoes
- 1/2 cup red onion, finely chopped
- 1 clove garlic, minced
- 1 teaspoon ground cumin
- 1 teaspoon chili powder
- Salt and pepper to taste
- 1 cup shredded cheese (cheddar, Monterey Jack, or a blend)
- Fresh cilantro or parsley for garnish
- Optional toppings: salsa, sour cream, avocado slices

Instructions:

Preheat Oven:
- Preheat your oven to 375°F (190°C).

Prepare Bell Peppers:
- Cut the bell peppers in half, removing the seeds and membranes. Place them in a baking dish.

Cook Quinoa:
- Cook the quinoa according to package instructions. Set aside.

Prepare Filling:
- In a large mixing bowl, combine the cooked quinoa, diced bananas, black beans, corn, diced tomatoes, red onion, minced garlic, ground cumin, chili powder, salt, and pepper. Mix well to combine.

Stuff Peppers:
- Spoon the quinoa and banana mixture into each bell pepper half, pressing down lightly to pack the filling.

Bake:
- Sprinkle shredded cheese over the top of each stuffed pepper. Cover the baking dish with aluminum foil.

Bake in Preheated Oven:
- Bake in the preheated oven for 25-30 minutes, or until the peppers are tender.

Broil (Optional):
- If you'd like to brown the cheese on top, you can broil the stuffed peppers for an additional 2-3 minutes, keeping a close eye to prevent burning.

Garnish and Serve:
- Remove from the oven and let the stuffed peppers cool slightly. Garnish with fresh cilantro or parsley. Serve with optional toppings like salsa, sour cream, or avocado slices.

Enjoy:
- Enjoy your Banana and Quinoa Stuffed Peppers as a wholesome and flavorful meal!

These stuffed peppers provide a delightful blend of sweetness from the bananas, heartiness from the quinoa, and a variety of textures and flavors from the other ingredients. It's a creative and nutritious twist on a classic dish.

Spicy Banana and Chicken Curry

Ingredients:

- 1.5 lbs boneless, skinless chicken thighs, cut into bite-sized pieces
- 2 ripe bananas, mashed
- 1 large onion, finely chopped
- 3 cloves garlic, minced
- 1 tablespoon ginger, grated
- 1 can (14 oz) diced tomatoes
- 1 can (14 oz) coconut milk
- 2 tablespoons curry powder
- 1 teaspoon ground cumin
- 1 teaspoon ground coriander
- 1/2 teaspoon turmeric
- 1/4 teaspoon cayenne pepper (adjust to taste for spice level)
- Salt and pepper to taste
- 2 tablespoons vegetable oil
- Fresh cilantro for garnish
- Cooked rice or naan for serving

Instructions:

Prepare Ingredients:
- Cut the chicken into bite-sized pieces, chop the onion, mince the garlic, and grate the ginger.

Sauté Chicken:
- In a large pot or Dutch oven, heat vegetable oil over medium-high heat. Add the chicken pieces and cook until browned on all sides. Remove the chicken from the pot and set it aside.

Sauté Onion, Garlic, and Ginger:
- In the same pot, add chopped onion and sauté until softened. Add minced garlic and grated ginger, cooking for an additional minute until fragrant.

Add Spices:
- Add curry powder, ground cumin, ground coriander, turmeric, and cayenne pepper to the pot. Stir well to coat the onions in the spices.

Cook with Tomatoes:

- Pour in the diced tomatoes with their juices. Stir and let it cook for a few minutes until the tomatoes start to break down.

Add Coconut Milk and Bananas:
- Pour in the coconut milk and add the mashed bananas to the pot. Stir to combine.

Return Chicken to Pot:
- Return the browned chicken pieces to the pot. Season with salt and pepper to taste. Stir well to coat the chicken in the curry mixture.

Simmer:
- Bring the curry to a simmer, then reduce the heat to low. Cover the pot and let it simmer for about 20-25 minutes, allowing the flavors to meld and the chicken to cook through.

Adjust Seasoning:
- Taste the curry and adjust the seasoning, adding more salt, pepper, or cayenne pepper if needed.

Serve:
- Serve the Spicy Banana and Chicken Curry over cooked rice or with naan. Garnish with fresh cilantro.

Enjoy:
- Enjoy your unique and flavorful Spicy Banana and Chicken Curry!

This curry offers a balance of sweetness from the bananas and heat from the spices, creating a delicious and aromatic dish. Adjust the spice level and sweetness according to your taste preferences.

Banana and Black Bean Quesadillas

Ingredients:

- 4 large flour tortillas
- 1 can (15 oz) black beans, drained and rinsed
- 2 ripe bananas, sliced
- 1 cup shredded cheese (cheddar, Monterey Jack, or a blend)
- 1/2 cup red onion, finely chopped
- 1/4 cup fresh cilantro, chopped
- 1 teaspoon ground cumin
- 1 teaspoon chili powder
- Salt and pepper to taste
- Olive oil or cooking spray for cooking

Optional Toppings:

- Guacamole
- Salsa
- Sour cream
- Lime wedges

Instructions:

Prepare the Black Bean Filling:
- In a bowl, combine black beans, sliced bananas, shredded cheese, chopped red onion, cilantro, ground cumin, chili powder, salt, and pepper. Mix well.

Assemble Quesadillas:
- Place a tortilla on a flat surface. Spread a generous portion of the black bean and banana mixture evenly over one half of the tortilla. Fold the other half over to create a half-moon shape.

Cook Quesadillas:
- Heat a skillet or griddle over medium heat. Lightly brush the surface with olive oil or use cooking spray. Place the quesadilla in the skillet and cook for 2-3 minutes on each side, or until the tortilla is golden brown and the cheese is melted.

Repeat:
- Repeat the process with the remaining tortillas and filling.

Slice and Serve:
- Once cooked, transfer the quesadillas to a cutting board and let them rest for a minute before slicing into wedges.

Optional Toppings:
- Serve the Banana and Black Bean Quesadillas with optional toppings like guacamole, salsa, sour cream, and lime wedges.

Enjoy:
- Enjoy your unique and flavorful Banana and Black Bean Quesadillas!

This combination of sweet bananas and savory black beans creates a delicious flavor profile. The quesadillas can be served as a snack, appetizer, or even a light meal. Customize the recipe by adding your favorite ingredients or adjusting the spice level to suit your taste preferences.

Banana and Avocado Salad

Ingredients:

- 2 ripe bananas, sliced
- 1 ripe avocado, diced
- 1 cup cherry tomatoes, halved
- 1/4 cup red onion, finely chopped
- 2 tablespoons fresh cilantro, chopped
- Juice of 1 lime
- Salt and pepper to taste
- Optional: Mixed salad greens (such as arugula or spinach)

Instructions:

Prepare Ingredients:
- Slice the bananas, dice the avocado, halve the cherry tomatoes, chop the red onion, and chop the fresh cilantro.

Assemble Salad:
- In a large bowl, combine the sliced bananas, diced avocado, halved cherry tomatoes, chopped red onion, and chopped cilantro.

Optional Greens:
- If you like, you can serve the salad on a bed of mixed salad greens for added freshness and texture.

Drizzle with Lime Juice:
- Squeeze the juice of one lime over the salad. The lime juice not only adds a zesty flavor but also helps prevent the bananas and avocados from browning.

Season:
- Season the salad with salt and pepper to taste. Gently toss the ingredients to coat them with lime juice and seasonings.

Serve:
- Serve the Banana and Avocado Salad immediately as a refreshing side dish or light lunch.

Enjoy:
- Enjoy this unique and delightful salad that combines the sweetness of bananas with the creamy texture of avocados!

This salad is a great way to showcase the contrasting flavors and textures of bananas and avocados. It's light, refreshing, and can be served on its own or as a side dish alongside grilled chicken or fish. Feel free to customize the salad by adding other fresh ingredients or a light vinaigrette if desired.

Banana and Cucumber Sushi Rolls

Ingredients:

- 1 cup sushi rice, cooked and seasoned with rice vinegar, sugar, and salt
- 1 nori (seaweed) sheet
- 1 ripe banana, peeled and sliced into thin strips
- 1/2 cucumber, julienned
- Soy sauce for dipping
- Pickled ginger and wasabi (optional, for serving)

Instructions:

Prepare Sushi Rice:
- Cook sushi rice according to package instructions. Season the cooked rice with a mixture of rice vinegar, sugar, and salt. Allow it to cool to room temperature.

Prepare Nori Sheet:
- Place a bamboo sushi rolling mat on a flat surface. Put a sheet of plastic wrap on top of the bamboo mat. Lay the nori sheet, shiny side down, onto the plastic wrap.

Spread Rice on Nori:
- Wet your hands to prevent the rice from sticking, and spread a thin layer of sushi rice evenly over the nori, leaving about 1 inch of the nori sheet uncovered at the top.

Add Banana and Cucumber:
- Arrange strips of banana and cucumber along the bottom edge of the rice.

Roll Sushi:
- Using the bamboo mat, start rolling the sushi from the bottom, tucking in the banana and cucumber as you go. Roll it tightly but not so tight that the filling squeezes out. Seal the edge with a little water.

Slice the Roll:
- With a sharp, wet knife, slice the sushi roll into bite-sized pieces.

Repeat (Optional):
- Repeat the process to make additional rolls.

Serve:
- Arrange the banana and cucumber sushi rolls on a serving platter.

Optional Garnish:

- Garnish with pickled ginger and wasabi if desired.

Dip and Enjoy:
- Serve with soy sauce for dipping and enjoy your Banana and Cucumber Sushi Rolls!

This sweet and refreshing sushi roll is a delightful treat. The combination of the creamy banana and crisp cucumber adds a unique flavor and texture to the sushi. It's a great option for those who enjoy experimenting with non-traditional sushi fillings.

Banana and Goat Cheese Crostini

Ingredients:

- Baguette or French bread, sliced into 1/2-inch thick rounds
- Olive oil for brushing
- 4 ounces goat cheese, softened
- 2 ripe bananas, sliced
- Honey for drizzling
- Fresh thyme leaves for garnish (optional)
- Pinch of sea salt (optional)

Instructions:

Preheat Oven:
- Preheat your oven to 375°F (190°C).

Prepare Crostini:
- Place the baguette or French bread slices on a baking sheet. Brush each slice lightly with olive oil on one side.

Toast Bread:
- Toast the bread slices in the preheated oven for about 8-10 minutes or until they are golden and crisp.

Spread Goat Cheese:
- Once the bread slices are toasted, spread a layer of softened goat cheese on the untoasted side of each slice.

Add Banana Slices:
- Place banana slices on top of the goat cheese layer.

Drizzle with Honey:
- Drizzle honey over the banana slices. The amount of honey can be adjusted based on your preference for sweetness.

Optional Garnish:
- If desired, sprinkle a pinch of sea salt and garnish with fresh thyme leaves for added flavor.

Serve:
- Arrange the Banana and Goat Cheese Crostini on a serving platter.

Enjoy:
- Serve immediately and enjoy this sweet and savory appetizer!

This combination of creamy goat cheese, sweet bananas, and the drizzle of honey creates a sophisticated and delicious flavor profile. The crostini are perfect for entertaining guests or as a unique addition to a charcuterie board. Feel free to experiment with additional toppings such as chopped nuts or a balsamic reduction for added complexity.

www.ingramcontent.com/pod-product-compliance
Lightning Source LLC
LaVergne TN
LVHW061938070526
838199LV00060B/3862